ENDORSEMENTS

We are indebted to Patricia Mays for providing us a "higher education" on "progressive education" in this book. *Truth in the Classroom* is insightful, convictional, and provocative. Readers who accept the challenge to think biblically when assessing America's public education will certainly begin to seek out more information, involvement, and alternatives. Even those without a Christian worldview will find her research and conclusions compelling and all worthy of an ethical response.

> Kenneth D. Polk, senior pastor
> Northside Baptist Church
> Murfreesboro, Tennessee

This book should be a "must" read for all persons who have concern for the educational process in America. This includes administrators, teachers, board members, and most of all parents and politicians. As an educator of forty years (public and private), I feel this book gets to the root of the problem we in America face. When reading the book, it is one you will not want to put down until every true word is read. I heartily endorse this book by Patricia Mays.

> Philip Back
> educator and retired administrator

TRUTH IN THE CLASSROOM

TRUTH IN THE CLASSROOM

THE IMPACT OF PROGRESSIVE EDUCATION
ON THE SOUL OF AMERICA

PATRICIA MAYS

TATE PUBLISHING & *Enterprises*

Published by Tate Publishing & Enterprises, LLC
127 E. Trade Center Terrace | Mustang, Oklahoma 73064 USA
1.888.361.9473 | www.tatepublishing.com

Tate Publishing is committed to excellence in the publishing industry. The company reflects the philosophy established by the founders, based on Psalm 68:11,
"The Lord gave the word and great was the company of those who published it."

Book design copyright © 2008 by Tate Publishing, LLC. All rights reserved.
Cover design by Jonathan Lindsey
Interior design by Stephanie Woloszyn

Published in the United States of America

ISBN: 978-1-60604-159-8
1. General Interest: Issues: Contemporary Social Issues (Education)
2. Christian Living: Practical Life: Contemporary Issues (Education)
08.05.01

DEDICATION

This book is dedicated first of all to the Lord Jesus Christ, who is the author of truth. It is also dedicated my husband, Bob, and our son, Andy, whose encouragement and support helped to make the work a reality. Bob spent many hours proofing and formatting the text. I would also like to thank my pastor, Ken Polk, for critiquing the book and for his fearless commitment to speaking the truth in love to his congregation.

TABLE OF CONTENTS

FOREWORD

In the 1960s we hit the wall, and we hit it hard in this nation. As we slid down the wall and found ourselves dog-paddling in the cesspool of situational ethics, free love, atheistic education, and "God is dead" theology, evangelical Christians seemed dazed and confused as to the condition in which we found ourselves. "How did we get to this condition?" seemed to be our anthem. Only a few prophetic voices from the Christian community had been warning us of our lethargic negligence to events that had begun in the 1920s and 1930s and had stealthily been permeating our culture. But today, some forty years past our collision, much of the Christian community still has not equated cause to effect, much less asked the critical question, "Is there a way to reverse the course of our cultural slide?" And still seemingly only a minority of Christians see the ravishment of a humanistic worldview and continue to sound the alarm with a clarion call to turn back to a Christian worldview.

In *Truth In The Classroom: The Impact of Progressive Education on the Soul of America,* Patricia Mays delivers a thorough, researched documentation of the "progressive" ideas as introduced into our public education by men such as Naturalist Charles Darwin, Philosopher John Dewey, and Educator Horace Mann, and also the generational effect we now experience some eighty-plus years later.

The author begins to masterfully examine the decay of absolute truth in our culture, as humanism and secularism have elevated man as the one who determines truth. Our national religion is humanism: by definition atheistic and by purpose the foundational philosophy of our public education. The author from this evidence begins to reveal that "what has been taking place in the classroom has indeed determined the direction of our society." From the changes in the fundamentals of teaching and tracking a student's progress to consequences in their lives both socially and morally…from the consequences to marriages and families…from our pulpits and pews, and finally to the major culture shift in our nation, all of this because we have abandoned the absolute truth of God's Word in the fabric of our public education system.

However, the author has not only left us with the historical diagnosis and present prognosis of our educational health. In what I believe is truly God-given inspiration, Patricia Mays gives us tangible, workable, and measurable methods that can turn our nation back to its foundation on the absolute truth of God's Word.

I believe that if, as the Bible says in John 8:31–32, the truth (absolute truth of God's Word) you know sets you free… then we as parents, grandparents, educators, Christians, and citizens of this nation must know the truth and then practice the truth. For this reason I believe this book is one of those "must read" and "must have" references for every parent or grandparent with pre-school and school-age children. I also believe pastors and all Christians need this book to be informed and aware of what is driving our culture.

Finally, on a personal note, as having the past privilege of being her pastor and working with her in the birth and nurturing of a Christian school, I know that Patricia Mays did not write this book as an exercise in academia but from years of personal experience with both public and private education and from a heart burdened and caring for a nation and for truth.

Kent Workman
retired pastor

INTRODUCTION

There is a prophecy in the Old Testament book of Daniel that in the end times truth will be thrown to the ground, and deceit will prosper (Daniel 8:12, 25).

In recent years Americans have become increasingly willing to give up on truth. Many now believe that truth can mean one thing to one person and something totally different to another. "You're okay, I'm okay," has become an established post modern philosophy. The notion of absolute, unchanging truth is anathema to some people, especially to many in academia. Often those who pride themselves on being the most highly enlightened among us are the most cynical when it comes to the idea of truth.

At the same time, we in the twenty-first century have convinced our collective selves that discipline is outdated. Spanking is out, but abortion is in. To spank your child is considered violence against him, but our society has determined that it is all right to kill him, brutally, with excruciating pain, if he is still in the womb. Capital punishment is out, but euthanasia is in. By today's standard for morality, cold-blooded murderers and savage child rapists should not be put to death, but it is okay to kill the severely handicapped and the infirm.

Dress codes for students are out. Anarchy is in. Gay and lesbian clubs on high school campuses are in, but any club or organization referring to Jesus must fight for existence. Creationism is out. Evolution is in. Schools are no longer permitted to suggest that there might be intelligent design in the formation of the universe. However, teachers can tell students that everything evolved from purely random, naturalistic means, and have the full support of the government behind them. The Pledge of Allegiance is out, unless the words "under God" are removed. Even a moment of silence has been challenged by liberal groups.

The Ten Commandments are out. Politically correct is in. Religious materials may not be displayed on government property, but politically and sexually offensive materials have been paid for with public money and displayed in government offices as "art." Monogamous, heterosexual marriage is out. Homosexuality and promiscuity are in. Restrictions on pornography and indecency on the airwaves are out. Sexual license is in.

At the same time, an alarming assault on language has taken place. Killing the unborn has become an issue of "individual rights." Respect for biblical marriage has become "homophobic" and "mean-spirited." Biblical Christianity has become "right-wing extremism." Special privileges for lawbreakers and those who refuse to act responsibly is known as "liberalism." "Tolerance" for all things offensive to biblical Christianity is considered compassionate.

There has definitely been a change in the American psyche and a rampant confusion about the meaning of truth. Many people believe that these changes have produced much that is destructive. Some even fear that the collapse of our civil and free society is swiftly approaching. It has become a much more dangerous time for all of us, and terrorism is only a small part of it. There may be far more to fear from within than without. It has been believed and spoken by many throughout our history that America's destruction could only come from a collapse of our character and virtues. We believed that no enemy would bring us down as long as we were strong in goodness. Though there is still much that is good about America, we have certainly fallen from the moral character that made us great. An important question to be asked is, "What brought us to this point?" One answer that can't be ignored is that much of what we see in a morally declining society has come from the subtle but unrelenting philosophies that became the foundation of our educational institutions.

As the progressive educational philosophy took root in the universities, along with it came an openness to communism, evolution, humanism, and secularism. These ideas at their foundation were in conflict with the beliefs held by most people in America at the beginning of the twentieth century. They certainly were and are inconsistent with biblical Christianity, and their growth would oppose any belief in absolute truth. The country would soon embrace a feel-good, self-promoting view of life which rejected any religious restraints on behavior.

The so-called "progressive" ideas were deliberately introduced into the public education system by people like John Dewey and Horace Mann. Following the advance of Darwin's theory of evolution with the Scopes Trial of 1925 and Alfred Kinsey's reports on human sexuality, morality in America began a nose dive from which it has not recovered. In some places sex education which embraces homosexuality now begins at the very earliest years of schooling.

The Kinsey Report on human sexuality was produced in a university setting and embraced as "scientific." It did more to promote the sexual revolution already taking place than perhaps any other factor. The result was to be the collapse of moral standards throughout the society.

Using the vehicle of evolution, the philosophies of humanism and secularism spread through the culture, bringing America into an era of skepticism and abandonment of faith in truth. It brought us to a time when everyone was supposed to find his own "truth" but be prevented from influencing others to believe it. It brought us to a time of great moral confusion and leanness in our souls. We are spiritually sick and getting sicker. We can no longer discern good from evil, and consequently are being consumed by the evil around and within us. We are currently a culture desperately in need of truth, for truth is always necessary in recognizing and dealing with evil.

> *"The time will come when men will not put up with sound doctrine. Instead, to suit their own desires, they will gather around them a great number of teachers to say what their itching ears want to hear."*
>
> (2 Timothy 4:3)

LOOKING FOR TRUTH IN EDUCATION

Can education which ignores truth be a noble enterprise?

When asked what it will take to solve the nation's problems, most Americans still put education at the top of the list. President Jimmy Carter must have believed schooling was essential for our preservation when he created the United States Department of Education with a 1980 budget of fourteen billion dollars, a figure that soared to nearly sixty billion dollars by 2003. Americans seem resigned to spending ever-increasing amounts of money to improve education, for we sense that the schooling of our children is of vital importance.

America is not alone in that sentiment. Every nation throughout recorded history has had an interest in education. The Bible addresses the training of children early in the book of Deuteronomy soon after the Exodus. Moses instructed the Israelites to teach diligently the commandments of God to their children so that they might live and prosper. The book of Proverbs echoes over and over the warning for young people to listen to instruction and to accept discipline in order to gain wisdom and understanding, so that it may be well with them.

Most people understand at least at some level that in order to continue, a society must pass on its values and ideals to future generations. To a great extent what takes place in the classroom will determine the direction of a society. Schools probably do more to shape the worldviews of our children than do any other influences they have. This unfortunately includes the family because in many cases children spend more time with teachers than they do with parents.

Abraham Lincoln noted that the philosophies of the classroom in one generation would be the philosophies of the government in the next. What we are taught affects how we think, and how we think determines what we will become. Despots and dictators know this well, and they always go after the minds of the young.

Hitler took over the schools of Germany to push his ideology, as did the Communists in the Soviet Union. Under Saddam Hussein Iraqi children spent much of their day reciting their dictator's propaganda. Much of the turmoil in the Middle East that spills over into terrorism comes from the fact that radical clerics have taught their brand of hatred for Israel and America to the youth there.

The ancient Greek philosopher Diogenes believed that "the foundation of any state is the education of its youth." The quote above is inscribed on an obelisk at a large state university in Indiana. Taken directly from an alumni newspaper from the same university was the following: "The great thinkers of ancient Greece, the philosophies of the Enlightenment, and the founding fathers of the United

States shared one belief: An essential building block of civilization is education." (1)

What, then, are valid purposes for education, what constitutes proper education, and who should be responsible for it? These are crucial questions, and the answers that emerge will depend on the worldviews of the ones who are asked.

Early Americans by and large had a biblical worldview. Beginning with the Puritans, education in America had noble intentions. Children were taught to read the Bible, using its lessons in right living to build strong character and encourage moral integrity. Universities were founded to train ministers who would continue to lead the nation, so that peace and blessings from God would be its heritage in years to come.

However, American education began a descent into troubled waters when philosophers and psychologists who were determined to redefine truth became leaders in education. They had a vastly different purpose in mind for schooling. These self-proclaimed pragmatists or "progressives" had come to the conclusion that truth is only a belief which people have agreed upon because it's what they desire. Therefore, "truth" could be changed to suit changing circumstances. The emerging "evidence" in favor of evolution made it easier for many of them to embrace atheism and reject the notion of absolute truth. In their minds teaching truth was no longer a valid purpose for education. However, they recognized the power of education to shape lives and to accomplish whatever vision they had in mind. They intended to lead the nation in a totally different direction from the one envisioned by its founders.

Early in the twentieth century, the philosophy of Communism was becoming quite popular among the upper class, especially those in academia. Communism promised a future utopia without the restrictions of religion. Former Communist, Whittaker Chambers, in his book *Witness,* stated that in the 1920s and 1930s, the "Communist National Students League was graduating its hundreds from the colleges." (2) He said that this made possible "the big undergrounds, the infiltration of the government, science, education, and all branches of communications." (3) He stated further that, "Nearly all (these Communist party members and infiltrators) were college trained from the top ten percent of their classes." (4)

The ideas that possibly had the greatest impact on the direction of education in this nation were those of John Dewey. Dewey had bought into the philosophy of pragmatism through his contact with the teachings of William James and other philosophers. The doctrine of pragmatism is that ideas are only valuable to the extent that they can produce desired results. The label "progressive" was a euphemism added to give legitimacy to the cause. Dewey was also heavily influenced by Charles Darwin's writings on evolution. Having abandoned any belief in absolute truth, it was a short step from there to his embracing evolution and atheism, basic ideologies underlying Communism. He became one of the leaders in the humanist movement, which elevated man to become determiner of his own truth and the god who would direct the future evolution of mankind.

From Dewey's many writings, it is almost impossible not to see his agreement with the Communist cause. He stated in one article published in the Nov./Dec., 1928, edition of the magazine *New Republic,* "The Russian educational situation is enough to convert one to the idea that only in a society based upon the cooperative principle can the ideals of educational reformers be adequately carried into operation." (5)

Agreeing with the supposed ideals of Communism, Dewey saw education's primary purpose as a means of social reform. He recognized the great potential of the education system for propaganda. If he and his followers were to create a new society, it would have to begin by changing the beliefs and the very soul of the nation. Therefore, he believed that education must necessarily become politicized. He and his colleagues recognized that if their vision were to become reality, the schools must take over more aspects of children's lives than traditional schooling had allowed. They needed politics and politicians to accomplish their utopian dream. Through the years they have succeeded in many if not most of their goals.

Dewey believed what most American Communists believed: that the individual is nothing, but the cause is everything. He and they believed that it was only through this means that all humanity could move to a higher level of existence, which would bring world peace through Communism.

As an educator of teachers, Dewey made sure his philosophies would make their way into the classrooms of America. His work and writings at the university level coupled with his leadership in the National Education Association gave him a powerful pulpit. No teacher trained at the university level in the past sixty years has failed to come into contact with Dewey's pragmatic, "progressive" ideas on education. His teachings and those of other like-minded educators have slowly but surely contaminated nearly every aspect of public education.

Another early influential American with views similar to Dewey's was Horace Mann who served as both a U.S. Senator and Secretary of Education for the State of Massachusetts. Mann was a Unitarian and believed strongly in the separation of education from religion. Mann also liked what he saw in the school systems of Communist countries. Although he embraced "moralistic" teachings in public schools, it must be remembered that the Unitarian position is one in which religious authority rests with the individual, not in the Bible or the person of Jesus Christ. Horace Mann had a great impact on the direction of public schools in America.

While the home should be the most important institution in forming the character and beliefs of children, the schools in America began to take over much more of that responsibility. As humanist philosophies grew in influence over educators, curriculum, and methods, America's traditional values and mores came under suspicion. The nation's children began to be indoctrinated with a new belief system. The influence of this change grew stronger with successive generations.

Many parents who spent great effort to teach their children their own values were baffled when those children returned from college having rejected all that their parents held dear. The worldview to which their children had been exposed through thirteen years of public school and four years of indoctrination at the university had swayed their thinking in a totally different direction from that of their parents and grandparents.

The values handed down from the founders of this nation, have been under attack almost since the beginning of the public school movement. Over the years there has been a subtle and gradual shift toward a different view of the world and humanity.

The basic difference in the worldview of America's founders and the prevailing view of our day is that they believed in human dignity based on the existence of a creator God. They believed in absolute truth revealed through his words recorded in the Bible, and in the sacrificial death and resurrection of his son Jesus Christ for all mankind. They believed every individual life is sacred to God and ultimately accountable to Him. In other words, they had a biblical worldview. Due to the humanistic influence on our culture through the schools, much of our society no longer accepts those beliefs. Humanists such as Dewey believed that valuing truth for truth's sake should be equated with superstition and therefore discarded. Dewey and his followers were determined to remove all Christian influence from the public schools. This was a necessary first step in removing those ideals from the whole of society.

For the greater part of our history, Americans embraced the ideals of the Christian faith. At first the attack on those beliefs was subtle, but in the last forty to fifty years, we have seen the Christian religion boldly attacked from all sides.

There have been relentless attempts to remove all symbols of the faith from the public conscience.

Speaking about the growing shift away from truth, Francis A. Schaeffer said in his book *A Christian Manifesto* that, "all of this has come about...through a fundamental change in the overall way people think and view the world and life as a whole." (6) Schaeffer rightly described the modern worldview as one based on a "material-energy, chance view of final reality." (7) It is obvious to any observing eye that this worldview is one based on the theory of evolution and spread throughout our culture via our education system.

Modern man declared the death of God and embraced evolution as the only absolute truth which can be known. The ramifications of this are the loss of our society's value base and confusion about right and wrong. Schaeffer saw no way that the Christian worldview and the modern one could ever co-exist. They are at war with each other and will continue to be until one or other wins out. Schaeffer said, "The humanists push for 'freedom,' but having no Christian consensus to contain it, that 'freedom' leads to chaos or to slavery under the state (or under an elite)." (8) History has shown that this is precisely what happened in Communist controlled countries.

Dr. James Dobson and Gary Bauer in their book *Children at Risk: The Battle For the Hearts and Minds of Our Kids* called this struggle a "great Civil War of Values." They went on to say, "For now the outcome is very much in doubt." (9)

The great question to be answered through this battle is whether we will acknowledge that there is ultimate truth and any valid basis for law, and if so, from where does it come. These are spiritual questions that are pertinent to all aspects of public life, for if all men have not been created with certain inalienable rights, we have no foundation for freedom.

There was a time in America when principles based upon Christianity and the Bible were the standard for morality. For most of our nation's history, this fact was recognized by the majority, including our elected leaders and the nation's judges. However, in more recent years, the increasingly successful push to secularize the nation has resulted in the rise of immorality to levels beyond anything our founders could have imagined. They could never have foreseen the culture of death that would spread like wildfire through our society, beginning with abortion on demand and leading right on up to the deliberate killing of the handicapped and infirm.

It has been rightly said that we have lost our moral compass. We are no longer able to agree on what morality is or whether we ought to even be a moral people. Though there are many factors that have contributed to the moral decline of the nation, the inescapable fact is a great deal of the blame for where we find ourselves surely belongs to our system of education.

The content and direction of education in America has for some time been under the control of the university rebels of the 1960s and 1970s who cast aside all that was held sacred in generations past. Those young men and women were the products of a flawed education that led them to believe they could and should remake the world in the image of a new god. They are now among our governors, senators, representatives, and judges. They are prominent in our news media. They are at the top levels of teachers' unions; they are running many of our universities and schools, and they are even among our clergy. They obviously are a majority among the entertainers and Hollywood crowd who have such a tremendous influence on our society.

Now that "progressives" have gained control over much of public opinion through political correctness, those who are leading the revolution have no intention of surrendering any of that power. The vehement opposition in this country to giving parents equal access to private and religious schools is precisely because it would inhibit the state's control over the minds of America's youth. The elites at the forefront of education believe that they have the right to determine the direction of our society, and they intend to do it through their increasing power over the schools. They see themselves and their philosophies as the real savior of mankind.

Although we have been assured that our nation's schools are and ought to be religion neutral, they certainly are not religion free. With the Scopes "monkey trial" of the 1920s, naturalistic evolution gained a firm foothold in the schools, despite the fact that much of what was accepted as evidence in its favor is now known to be fraudulent. With the inevitable atheistic dogma that accompanies evolution, it was assured that future laws would further ban Christian thought and expression from the classroom. However, another religion rose quickly to fill the void.

Humanism became the new religion of our public schools. It would have us look to our own hearts to define righteousness. On the other hand, the Bible warns, "He who trusts in himself is a fool" (Proverbs 28:26). Sadly, even Christians often tell children to look into their hearts to find what is good. However, the truth according to the Bible is that, "the heart is deceitful above all things and beyond cure" (Jeremiah 17:9). Our founders recognized the sinful nature of man, and they knew that if we were to continue to have a free society, our children must be taught the truth. They understood that children must have a moral and religious education. However, the public education system fell into the hands of those who had different ideas and a vastly different purpose in mind.

First Lady Hillary Clinton in her book claimed that "it takes a village" to raise a child properly. Similar sentiments come to us from many public leaders. Mrs. Clinton did not have in mind the extended family of grandparents, uncles and aunts along with Sunday school teachers and other church influences on children. What she really meant was that the responsibility for education and much of child rearing should belong to the government, and that government must decide both the purpose and direction of schooling for our children. She meant that state superintendents or commissioners of education could place a child's "right" to get an abortion or drug counseling above a parent's right to know what is happening in their children's lives. Because Americans have accepted a constantly expanding role of government to provide for them, they have surrendered many of their God-given responsibilities for their children to the government.

There is no question that the government has become increasingly more intrusive into the family and the raising of children. Parents are placing their children at younger and younger ages into government-sponsored day care programs. Schools are taking children at three and four years of age. Before school and after school programs keep children for longer and longer portions of the day. Year-round schools are becoming ever more popular, and schools offer programs for children even during their vacation times. Health care for children is being linked to the schools through family resource centers and youth services centers. Counseling and psychological intervention for students are now offered through most schools.

We are told by our government leaders that these programs are more necessary than ever, and consequently must have more funding. Why? Because our children are not getting proper care at home, they say. Therefore, the government must step up and provide what is missing so that every child has an equal chance in life. But is the government really making our children's lives better through education, or has the government contributed to creating the problems in the first place? One needs only to look at the condition of our society for the answer.

Authorities are now dealing with crimes of drug use, assault, rape, and murder in the nation's schools. In recent years there has been a growing problem with sexual exploitation of students by their teachers. There have been multiple incidents of students killing classmates and teachers. In 1997 a student in Paducah, Kentucky, opened fire on a group of young people gathered for prayer before school. Three of his classmates died and five others were wounded.

In 1999 two teenagers in Middleton, Colorado, shocked the nation by killing a dozen of their classmates and a teacher before turning their guns on themselves. Bodies of the victims could not be removed from the school for many hours because of the nearly fifty bombs the killers had planted. The nation watched in horror as scenes of the situation were played over and over again on their televisions.

In both Middleton and Paducah, it seemed that students who publicly prayed or professed faith in God were singled out for destruction. However, in both cases, people of faith were later called upon to lead in drawing the broken communities together to begin the healing process. Tremendous testimonies of faith were broadcast across the nation on prime time. There were renewed efforts to post the Ten Commandments in schools. However, even some professing Christians denounced such action as a danger to the constitutional separation of church and state.

The questions, "What has happened to our schools?" and "what can we do to change it?" would be asked over and over again on TV talk shows for weeks and months to follow. The answer is clear to those who have seen this coming for the past generation.

The nation has lost its moral compass because our children are being taught in classrooms devoid of morality and virtue. Because of new interpretations on the separation of church and state, all acknowledgment of divine authority has been banned from public education. When divine authority is denied, all other authority becomes relative. Respect for any kind of authority begins to erode. When "values" are taught at all in today's public schools, they are based on the shifting sand of moral relativism and political correctness. In such a moral climate, when young people are told they shouldn't behave in certain ways, of course their answer will be, "Says who?"

The state has taken over the job of parenting and ordered that our children be taught in a religion-neutral atmosphere. Consequently, the moral foundations of our society are collapsing around us.

In Roberts v. Madigan the court ruled in 1989 that public school teachers could not keep religious (Christian) books in the classroom, and a teacher could not silently read his own copy of the Bible in the presence of his students. In June of 2000, the United States Supreme Court struck down voluntary student-led prayer before sporting events. A court in California determined just after the turn of the millennium that reciting the Pledge of Allegiance in public schools is unconstitutional unless the words "under God" are removed.

While prayer and the Bible have been removed from our schools, our children are being taught through sex education classes that homosexuality, sadomasochism, and even pedophilia are acceptable behaviors. On June 20, 2000, the Christian Broadcasting Network aired parts of a secretly taped sex education conference in Massachusetts where teachers were clearly heard telling children as young as fourteen how to perform deviant sex acts. The conference had been facilitated with help from the Department of Education in the state. (It should be no surprise that the courts of Massachusetts opened the way in 2004 for same sex marriage to have equal footing with traditional marriage.)

This is happening in a nation which was founded on biblical Christianity and whose very freedoms were based upon the laws contained in the Ten Commandments. Today the Ten Commandments have not only been barred from schools but from other public buildings as well.

Many Americans alarmed by the increasing breakdown of our society want morals and ethics to be returned to our schools. However, the inevitable question is: Whose morals and ethics should be taught, and on what should those be based? In the beginning of this nation, there was a Christian consensus, and there was no question that the morals taught to our children would come from the Bible. When the Bible has been barred as the final authority all that is left is political correctness. Since this is an untrustworthy and changing source, America is currently incapable of dealing with the problem in any worthwhile or lasting way. It all boils down to the question of whether or not there is objective, unchanging truth, and if so, from whom does it come. Those who are leading our public institutions of learning have said there is no such truth, many of our political and even religious leaders have agreed, and our society is paying the price.

Recent surveys have shown that a majority of Americans continue to claim to be Christian. However, the surveys have also found that most of those same Americans do not have a true biblical worldview because they know very little about real biblical Christianity. A majority say the Ten Commandments are still valid rules for living, but they are hard pressed to name two or three. No doubt, if they did know more about them, many Americans would feel it necessary to subject some of those commandments to redefinition.

On his July 13, 2000, radio broadcast, Dr. James Dobson quoted from a recent Gallup poll of teenagers. The poll found that only twenty percent of the teens could answer even one of three very basic questions about the Christian religion. The questions were: 1) How many disciples did Jesus have? 2) What are the four gospels in the New Testament? 3) What religious event is commemorated at Easter? We have become a nation of biblical illiterates, and our children are inheriting a rapidly decaying civilization. According to researcher, George Barna, even most young people being raised in Christian homes will abandon the faith of their parents when they reach adulthood.

Discussing the spiritual quest of America's teenagers, a writer for *Newsweek* called today's youth "more spiritual than their parents but often less conventionally so…putting together their own religious canon as they would a salad from a salad bar." (10) The author went on to say, "For the bulk of the nation's twenty-two million teenagers, religion and spirituality entail a quest not for absolute truths but for ways to live among relative truths." (11) When surveyed, the majority of these individuals confessed that their interest in spirituality has had little impact upon their behavior. They are interested in religion, but not necessarily the Christian religion. They want an impersonal god, one they can call on if they are in need, but one who will not put limits on their behavior.

Reporting on a study by "the New York-based Inter-religious Information Center," Elaine Fletcher wrote for Religion News Service that, "Americans increasingly perceive religion as a personal quest rather than a binding social force." (12) She suggested that true Christianity is very much on the decline in this nation.

Based on a Campus Crusade for Christ study, a Southern Baptist newspaper reported that eighty-eight percent of teens do not attend church and that up to eighty percent of those who do will drop out after their high school graduation. (13) All over the country more and more students are rejecting the notion of absolute truth, and much of their cynicism can be traced right back to the schoolhouse door. What will be the impact on our nation when these young people take their places as America's leaders?

There is a critical need to raise up a generation of young people who know the truth, the unchanging, absolute truth, who will be salt and light to a dying world through a personal relationship with Jesus Christ. However, we cannot expect to see this happen when the spiritual training of our children, even in committed Christian homes, may consist of an hour or two of church weekly. They might even get a week or two of Bible school during the summer, and maybe a couple of retreats during the adolescent years (much of which will be of a social or entertaining nature).

We must remember that children in public schools are exposed to a secular worldview for six or seven hours a day for around 180 days a year. With extended school days, months, and years, as is being proposed by most reformers, it will be even more. That worldview will be even further solidified through the movies and television they watch, and the music to which they listen. Unfortunately, it may even be advanced by their church leaders and Christian teachers who bought into wrong philosophies through their own education at liberal universities.

Education is indeed crucial to civilization, but does knowledge alone hold the power to solve our nation's problems and those of the world? Education reformers rejected knowledge as the basis for learning long ago, claiming that it was critical thinking and social learning that would bring peace and security to the world. However, it is important to ask whether any education can bring lasting answers apart from God. To find the answer to that question, one need go no further than the book of Ecclesiastes in the Bible. Solomon was said to be the wisest man who ever lived. Besides his wisdom, he had wealth, power, victory over his enemies, creative abilities, everything the world has to offer, and he indulged himself to the maximum in all of them. In describing his accomplishments, he said:

> I became greater by far than anyone in Jerusalem before me…I denied myself nothing my eyes desired; I refused my heart no pleasure. Yet when I surveyed all that my hands had done and what I had toiled to achieve, everything was meaningless, a chasing after the wind.
>
> (Ecclesiastes 2:7–11)

> He said of learning, "The fate of the fool will overtake me also. What then do I gain by being wise?"
>
> (Ecclesiastes 2:15)

In the end he learned this:

> Of making many books there is no end; and much
> study wearies the body. Here is the conclusion of the
> matter: Fear God and keep his commandments, for
> this is the whole duty of man. For God will bring
> every deed into judgment, including every hidden
> thing, whether it is good or evil.
>
> (Ecclesiastes 12:13–14)

What Solomon discovered is still true today. No matter how great the knowledge or the power, apart from God it will solve nothing. The real problem with the human condition is a spiritual one.

Whittaker Chambers' long and tortuous escape out of Communism brought him to the conclusion that "religion begins at the point where reason and knowledge are powerless and forever fail—the point at which man senses the mystery of his good and evil, his suffering and his destiny as a soul in search of God." (14) He says further "I did not understand that the malady of life around me…and the malady of the life of my family…were different manifestations of the same malady—the disorder that overtakes societies and families when a world has lost its soul." (15) He claimed, "The dying world of 1925 was without faith, hope, character…it had lost the power to distinguish between good and evil." (16)

Several things happened after the 1920s, including exposure of Communist espionage at the highest levels of America's government and another world war, which seemed to slow the advance of the humanist take-over. However, it wasn't dead, and soon rose to prominence again. It was still at work in our colleges and universities as well as among our education policy makers and politicians.

Totalitarian regimes, some highly regarded among many of America's liberals, made no secret of the fact that the schools must play a very important part in spreading their propaganda. These regimes recognized also that the family was a very real hindrance to their cause, since it also affected the mentality and psychological attitudes of the future generations. Therefore, it was to their advantage to break down the family unit wherever possible. This purge of the family was to get its stranglehold on America through no-fault divorce, abortion on demand, lifting of restrictions on pornography, acceptance of homosexuality, and an exodus of moms from the home to the marketplace. We are facing a redefining of the roles of husband and wife and changing values regarding marriage and sex that increasingly assault the sanctity and stability of the home. Most Americans do not realize that this moral breakdown has been planned and orchestrated by a powerful elite through their influence over education, law, and government. It was inevitable that the secular, naturalistic thinking being taught in the universities would make its way into religious institutions as well.

In the past fifty years, there have been hundreds of documented cases of sexual abuse by the clergy. One of the biggest issues of the Catholic Church in our generation has been sexual abuse of children by priests. It should have been no surprise that the Episcopal church of New Hampshire was among the first to elect an openly homosexual bishop. Americans have lost touch with the concept of sin, and people are now offended by use of the term. Public schools certainly cannot teach children about sin, and many churches no longer preach it.

Our nation has been indoctrinated for the past seventy years or more with a philosophy that says people are born basically good and are only corrupted by society. Children are taught from elementary school all the way through the university that man evolved from mindless matter by mere chance, that people are just higher animals on the evolution tree. That belief leads naturally to the conclusion that there is no absolute standard for truth, and that people determine what is moral and ethical based on their own thinking. Our education has had a great influence on what we believe and what we call truth. These ideas have become the religious philosophy of the nation and have led naturally to the moral breakdown of our society.

Many of the worst criminals in our land today are among the most educated. A few years ago, a local paper carried an article about a fifty-year-old Harvard law school graduate who had been a successful lawyer in the area, but was now facing a second trial on charges of possessing a forged instrument and theft. He had already been convicted in the first trial and was serving time. This man allegedly lied to clients about settlements they received and then kept more than he was supposed to. The news article stated that he had "earned advanced degrees in banking, law and public service," and was currently working as "an executive director for the American Education Network Corp., a non-profit organization based in Massachusetts." (17) This man's education obviously had failed to provide him with moral character.

A top education official in the state of Kentucky was forced to resign in the 1990s amid allegations of embezzling and money laundering. She was accused of diverting 1.2 million dollars of state tax money into accounts controlled solely by her. Deputy Commissioner Randy Kimbrough pled guilty to embezzling half a million dollars of state education funds. She admitted creating fifty fictitious consultants and having their paychecks sent to her. Not only that, but she had the state pay her husband $175,000 for consulting fees. Co-workers were shocked by the revelations. She was held in high regard by the Department of Education. Her credentials included advanced degrees in education and many years of experience as an education leader.

At about the same time as the Kimbrough affair, there were two other top education officials facing indictment in the state of Kentucky for theft of public funds. The auditor assigned to investigate the Kimbrough case concluded that the Department of Education itself had allowed "a culture that encourages circumventing and in some cases violating law and regulations." (18)

Kentucky was one of the first states to fall prey to a massive take-over of the schools by proponents of the progressive education philosophy. The entire education system was thrown out and re-created under reforms in 1990. Top education officials acted as if they had been given a license to do whatever they wanted. There was an attitude of arrogance that resulted in squelching any criticism of the reforms and efforts to control public opinion through endless propaganda. However, in spite of attempts to excuse and cover up, many failures and outright abuses such as those mentioned eventually did surface. Not only that, but the educational changes set student performance of basic skills back a long way. Because of the state's control over testing methods and means used to interpret and publish scores, the decline would not be obvious for many years.

Kentucky's experience is just a microcosm of what happens when a group with flawed philosophies gains control over the system, and it is an important reminder that education alone, and especially one embedded in secular humanistic philosophy, has no real answers to moral problems. Such a system has abandoned the search for truth and therefore no longer offers a valid education.

"If you hold to my teaching, you are really my disciples. Then you will know the truth, and the truth will set you free."

(John 8:31b-32)

Truth and Liberty, the Connection

Is there danger in forgetting the source of freedom?

America's founders referred to God at least three times in that famous, world-changing document called the Declaration of Independence. They firmly stated, "We hold these Truths to be self-evident, that all Men are created equal, that they are endowed by their Creator with certain inalienable Rights, that among these are Life, Liberty and the Pursuit of Happiness." They went on to say, "We, therefore, the Representatives of the United States of America, in general Congress assembled, appealing to the Supreme Judge of the world for the rectitude of our intentions, do…publish and declare that these United Colonies are, and of right ought to be, free and independent States…" The declaration ended with these words: "And for the support of this Declaration, with a firm Reliance on the Protection of divine Providence, we mutually pledge to each other our Lives, our Fortunes, and our sacred Honor." These men knew the horrors of tyranny, and they understood that the stand they were taking could well cost them their fortunes and their lives. Their writings show that they believed that liberty comes from God, and that they must rely on his protection. They knew that forgetting the source of liberty would lead to its loss.

The framers of our constitution were totally dedicated to freedom, but they also had an understanding of the responsibilities that go along with it. They recognized that there is no such thing as unrestricted freedom. They knew that because of the fallen nature of mankind, freedom cannot exist without restraints. They saw government as essential in preserving freedom for all. The founders also understood that legitimate government begins with God who created man to be free, and such a government must follow his dictates in order to succeed. This does not mean that they intended to form a theocracy. Far from it. They embraced freedom for everyone to practice religion as they chose. They understood that true Christianity has to be an individual decision. It cannot be forced on anyone. However, they did recognize that only Christianity was based on solid, complete, and unchanging truth. Therefore, our government must follow its principles if it were to be a lasting and peaceful one.

John Jay, one of the original Supreme Court Justices said, "The most effectual means of securing the continuance of our civil and religious liberties is always to remember with reverence and gratitude the source from which they flow." (1) George Washington stated, "Religion and morality are the essential pillars of civil society." (2)

The original constitution for Connecticut, known as the "Fundamental Orders of Connecticut" stated in part, "… there should be an orderly and decent government established according to God." (3) Founding Father, James Otis, wrote,

"...the sum of my argument is that civil government is of God." (4) Benjamin Franklin, though not a professing Christian, said, "Religion restrains bad behavior." (5) From Franklin's other writings, it is obvious he was referring to the Christian religion. Robert Winthrop, Speaker of the U.S. House said in an 1849 speech to the Massachusetts Bible Society, "Men, in a word, must necessarily be controlled either by a power within them or by a power without them; either by the Word of God or by the strong arm of man; either by the Bible or by the bayonet." (6)

Though revisionists of history deny it, it is obvious from the founders' own words that the majority of them were not only familiar with the Bible, but they accepted its authority. They intended to base the new government on its principles, and they wanted to be sure that future generations would be vigilant to preserve that heritage. For that reason they wanted an educated citizenry, one that could read and think critically to discern the truth. The nation would have to produce citizens that not only could but would read the founding documents and be able judge future laws and decisions accordingly. They recognized education as an ally to a free society, but only if it were education based on discerning and knowing the truth.

From the earliest days of the nation, schools were established to teach children reading, writing, and arithmetic. Furthermore, the founders realized that no education would be sufficient without instruction in righteousness. In many early American schools, the only textbook was the Bible. As other books were added, they included morals based on teachings from the Scriptures. Authors such as Noah

Webster made sure that their books preserved the Christian heritage of his beloved United States of America.

God richly blessed America in its early days, and for the next two hundred years the nation grew and prospered as no other nation in history. From all over the world, people who longed for freedom and a better life flocked to America.

However, just as the children of Israel forgot that God was their source of liberty, Americans lost touch with the fact that this nation was founded on the principles of God's Word and has endured by God's protection. Both Moses and Joshua gave instructions to Israel about how to continue in God's favor as a nation and what the consequences of abandoning their covenant with Him would be. Despite their warnings, future generations failed to be watchful. They didn't rehearse God's laws in the ears of their children, and the time came when their rulers did not even know what those laws were. Their people embraced paganism, their society was falling apart, and they were heading toward judgment from God.

The book of God's law had been lost for years before it was found in the temple, and Judah's King Josiah was introduced to it. When he heard for the first time the words written in the book, King Josiah was struck with the realization of his nation's sin and terrified by the impending judgment it called for. He immediately embarked on a mission to cleanse the nation of all its idols and to acquaint the people with God's commandments. In response to Josiah's repentance and desire to follow God, the nation was not destroyed during his lifetime. However, the Bible records that Judah's eventual destruction was certain because

King Manasseh had "filled Jerusalem with innocent blood; and the Lord was not willing to forgive" (2 Kings 24:3–4). The preceding chapters describe some of those innocents as the children who were sacrificed to demons. Judgment came to Judah, and the people lost all their freedoms when they became slaves to the Babylonians.

We in America have come to a time when many of our leaders don't seem to know (or care to know) what is right. Though they may use religious sounding platitudes for talking points, many have no true concern about God or his judgments, and our children are being sacrificed. Proverbs tells us that, "When the righteous thrive, the people rejoice; when the wicked rule, the people groan" (Proverbs 29:2). We are in a time of mourning in this nation, mourning for our children being killed in their schools, gunned down in the streets, and slaughtered in the womb. Sexual predators stalk the land, and children are no longer safe in their own beds. The violence in this country has been escalating at a dizzying speed over the past several years. We have to ask ourselves what has brought us to this point.

For the greater part of our history, Americans recognized the need to elect leaders who acknowledged a fear of God. They examined the character of potential leaders and looked for honesty, integrity, and moral behavior. Though there have always been some bad people who were crafty enough slip through the cracks of our political system, most citizens understood that we had to have good people in government. People recognized the truth that a person who does not have a fear and awe of God, has no real standard for doing what is right. They cannot be trusted to make unselfish and difficult decisions. Perhaps many of them had been taught the words from Proverbs, "He whose walk is upright fears the Lord, but he whose ways are devious despises him" (Proverbs 14:2). The Bible also states that, "Evil men do not understand justice, but those who seek the Lord understand it fully" (Proverbs 28:5).

Where and when did the American concept of right and wrong become so awash with "politically correct" ideas and so far from biblical truth? There is no doubt that much of it has come about and taken root through the philosophical foundations of our system of education called public schools. Parents handed over their God-given responsibility for the teaching of their children to a system that says that education and religious instruction are incompatible, a system that says we have no standard for truth. We have sown the wind, and we are reaping the tornado (Hosea 8:7). Timothy speaks of people who are "always learning but never able to acknowledge the truth" (II Timothy 3:7). Americans spend increasingly more on providing education without regard for truth. Consequently, the nation's problems only seem to escalate, and the promised utopia is nowhere in sight.

Dr. Benjamin Rush, one of the youngest signers of the Declaration of Independence, said "The only foundation for a useful education in a republic is to be laid in religion. Without this there can be no virtue, and without virtue there can be no liberty." (7) George Washington signed the Northwest Ordinance in 1789 encouraging schools in Illinois to teach "religion, morality, and knowledge." (8) Washington said, "True religion affords to government its surest support." (9) John Adams believed that religion and the morality built on it were the only foundations of "republicanism and of all free governments." (10)

After seventy years without religious instruction, the collapsing Russian society began to welcome Bible teachers back, and even allowed Bibles to be distributed in schools. Can anyone seriously doubt that they saw a connection between the breakdown of their society and the lack of a moral foundation like that given in the Bible? We must wonder how much destruction of our own society it will take to bring America to a recognition of our need to return to biblical principles. If we do not teach these to our children, the freedoms won for us through the sacrifices of our founders and all those who have given their lives to protect it will eventually be lost to them.

An essential starting place in changing the direction of our society must be with education, for the corruption that took place in our educational system bears a great deal of the responsibility for where we are as a nation. When the education leaders became men and women who embraced humanism, truth was thrown to the ground. Let no one mistake the fact that a humanist cannot be one who believes in God. The very definition of humanism by its leading proponents gives no place for belief in the supernatural. They believe that man and the universe are the highest forms of existence. They believe that only man can be his own god. Where does this place them in regard to their philosophy of government?

Humanists embraced the same philosophies as Marx and Lenin. Communists were essentially atheists, and so are humanists. They believed that only man can order the universe, and that the best way to do so is through socialism. Marx saw democracy as pitting one section of the population against another. However, both he and Lenin saw the state as a necessary evil in the transition between capitalism and communism. They believed that man was on an evolutionary path that would lead to a utopian society, at which time they would no longer need states or governments. Their stated desire was to abolish all classes so that all wealth could be held equally, but in reality their ambitions led inevitably to dictatorships. One of the first goals of communist dictatorships was to abolish religion. Mass persecution always followed the institution of a communist state. The freedom of religion was the first enemy of the state to be defeated under these dictatorships. All other freedoms had to be subordinated to the "party." Individuals were unimportant. The "cause" was all that mattered. History has shown that this ideology has been perhaps the most ruthless ever to arise. It has been estimated that the lives of over two hundred million people were sacrificed in this experiment.

The founders of our beloved country recognized freedom as a gift from Almighty God and that as such it must go hand in hand with truth. Our nation in the past generation has denied children access to truth through our schools. In its place they have substituted humanism, evolution, and moral relativism. However, God-given freedom can never be separated from truth, and those who try to do so face destructive consequences.

Without truth people begin to think of freedom as something it is not. They see freedom as the absence of constraints. They believe there should be no restrictions on their desires or consequences for their actions. Any rational person should be able to see that freedom without responsibility to others leads to chaos and confusion, but that is precisely the point where America has arrived. That is why we can no longer tolerate the Ten Commandments. That is why we now are forced to consider an amendment to our constitution that would protect the kind of marriage that has been the foundation for civilization throughout history.

One of the greatest responsibilities of education should always be to present truth. Jesus said his people, the ones who held to his teaching, would know the truth, and the truth would set them free (John 8:32). The truth has been kept from our children, and their freedoms are in great jeopardy. Democracy cannot work without the truth. Where there is no fear of God, the worst of man's nature will take over. Pride, self-centeredness, greed, and lust will pit man against man in such a world. Man who has no belief in eternal reward or punishment will never be able to love his neighbor as himself. Eternal vigilance is crucial to the well-being of a free society, but how can we keep watch over the truth if we no longer know what it is or how to find it?

Our education gurus, especially at the university level, have declared that the material cosmos is all that exists, and that it basically created itself. Therefore, they believe that objective truth does not exist. Morals and values and thoughts about a loving Creator are all figments of man's mind, they reason, so one person's values are as good as another's. If this is the case, then whoever wields the most power determines the extent of individual freedoms. This atheistic naturalism is the essence of Communism and Fascism, which willingly imprison or kill off whole groups of people who disagree with the philosophy. Let no one miss the fact that this kind of thinking grew and prevailed on many college and university campuses in America until Christianity has been effectively erased from our educational system. Humanism is the only religion left to those who reject God, and it is in direct conflict with the Declaration of Independence, which states that we have been endowed with certain rights by our Creator. The founders recognized liberty for all as an enduring truth which is "self-evident."

It is no coincidence that at the same time that Christianity was being erased from the American education system, so was the emphasis on our founding documents. Students in our nation had for most of our history been required to read the Declaration of Independence, the Constitution, and other important documents. They were taught to memorize portions and were given written tests during several years of their schooling. In his book *Original Intent*, David Barton cited a Department of Education report in recent years which stated that less than five percent of high school juniors and seniors even have the skills necessary to comprehend a primary-source historical document. This agrees with several polls taken of college students which show them to be woefully ignorant of American history. When people in this country are continually told that the Constitution requires a separation of religion and government, how can they refute it when they don't know what the document really says?

Americans no longer understand the truth about the

foundations for our government. Most students in the nation could not explain the difference between a democracy and a republic. They have not been taught that the founders did not trust a democracy that was open to the whims of the people; "mobocracy" as they saw it. On the other hand, a republic was one based upon laws. The founders recognized that for any law to be legitimate, it had to conform to standards that were consistent with natural law and with God's laws as found in the Bible, standards which would not change, but remain universal in operation for the good of the whole community.

If God is true and the Bible his revealed Word, it is for all people and for every part of their lives throughout all ages. It cannot be both true and at the same time be irrelevant to education, to science, to politics, to sociology, to law, or any other life issue. The question must be asked, "Is any education apart from the truth worth having?" Is such an education something we should want for our children? Moreover, abandoning the truth and attempting to build a society on false foundations will inevitably lead to chaos and the collapse of that civilization.

Moral breakdown leads to unrestrained violence, which threatens the freedoms of every individual in a society. One cannot read a newspaper or watch television news without being confronted with the increasing level of violence in America.

The recent violence in America's schools is one symptom of the spiritual vacuum in which our children are being raised. Many parents are now afraid to send their children to school. Some schools use police officers to monitor halls, and some have placed metal detectors at the doors and cameras throughout the building. Schools are focusing on safety as much or possibly more than curriculum. Some schools are issuing identification badges to students, requiring uniforms or stricter dress codes that would ban baggy clothing that could conceal weapons, and insisting on see-through plastic book bags. Alternative programs and locations for students with discipline problems are becoming more prevalent.

Schools are not the only unsafe places for our children. The streets of some of our cities are now so bad that taxis will not even go through them. In some neighborhoods, the biggest threat to childhood safety is gang warfare and drive-by shootings. Tourists must think twice about visiting America, which may have become one of the most violent countries in the world.

Pundits have offered a myriad of ideas on what and who is to blame for this dismal state of affairs. Many point the finger at the easy availability of handguns. However, Americans have always had guns. Obviously, guns make it easier to kill people, but, to paraphrase Archie Bunker, "Would it make us feel any better if these violent students were pushing their victims out of windows?" Most likely such deeply troubled children would find a way to vent their murderous rage with or without guns. If the bombs planted in the Columbine High School had gone off as planned, there would have been many times more casualties. The terrible bombings of the federal building in Oklahoma and the World Trade Center, and obviously the carnage of the Twin Towers on September 11, 2001, did not involve guns.

Several have suggested that violence in movies and video

games bears some responsibility for the increase in school violence, and a few hint at low self-esteem, child abuse, poverty, and any number of other social ills. One syndicated columnist put the blame for students "harassing, verbally abusing and physically threatening teachers...squarely on the shoulders of parents because they neither discipline their children nor allow school authorities to discipline them." (11)

When some of the residents from the towns affected by fatal school shootings got together as a group to discuss ways to prevent tragedies like that from happening, they agreed that prevention has to start at home. They suggested that parents must become totally familiar with their child's room, looking for posters, music, videos, books, and any kind of information with anti-social themes. It was further suggested that teachers, coaches, bus drivers, and others watch for such signals. Any suggestion that the parents of some of these teens were to blame, though, has been questioned, because some of the worst offenders came from "model homes" by today's standards. Theirs were two-parent homes with parents in highly respected positions in the community. Some were involved in community service and even described as church-goers.

The family as the hub of civilized society is under attack as never before. In past generations it was understood that the job of schools was to support the family in the raising of their children. Education was to follow the dictates of the home and respect the shared values that hold the society together. As the family goes, so goes the nation. Liberals and deviant groups have used the schools to promote their own agendas, agendas that attack traditional values and lead to the disintegration of the family as it was ordained by God. They actively promote through the schools the acceptance of homosexual marriage and the raising of children in such homes. They also promote promiscuity and abortion. If they succeed in destroying the biblical model for the family, they will succeed in destroying America.

It is hard to imagine how anyone could justify allowing the gruesome practice of partial birth abortion to continue. It's just as hard to understand how a country like Germany could reach the point of systematically murdering millions of Jews and other "undesirables" according to their government. However, it happened because the people of that country had entered a time of moral bankruptcy much like the one America has entered. If the trend toward the cheapening of life continues in this nation, and the church does not rise up to sound the alarm, we will surely follow in the steps of the Nazis.

In a 1998 article in the "Focus On The Family News From Dr. James Dobson," Albert Einstein was quoted concerning the rise of the Nazi revolution. He said,

Being a lover of freedom…I looked to the universities to defend (freedom), knowing that they had always boasted of their devotion to the cause of truth; but no, the universities were immediately silenced. Then I looked to the great editors of the newspapers whose flaming editorials in days gone by had proclaimed their love of freedom; but they, like the universities, were silenced…

Mr. Einstein was uncovering a revolutionary change in the mindset of universities that would take their students further and further from the ideal of truth, and therefore further from the ideal of freedom. The universities and the newspapers by and large in this country have failed to defend human life in recent decades. Instead they have been assisting the growth of attitudes that would threaten the most vulnerable and defenseless among us.

Though the death of freedom in this nation struck first at the unborn, it has not stopped there. Already we have seen the courts sentence a young handicapped woman to death by dehydration and starvation because she could not speak for herself. We have seen the courts declare that cities can seize the rightful property of citizens in order to use it to promote economic growth. Individuals have been told that they cannot speak about religious convictions in certain public settings, particularly in school and university classrooms. Ministers are told that use of certain politically charged words from the pulpit could cause their churches to lose tax exempt status. We are no longer allowed to display the Ten Commandments in court houses or schools. Prayer before state and federal events has been silenced. Pro-life demonstrators are not allowed to peacefully protest before abortion clinics.

Freedom cannot long endure in a nation that does not recognize its source. A government that can rule that the unborn are not fully human can also rule that some other group is not fully human and therefore has no rights. We now recognize the injustice done to African Americans through our courts in the past, but we have now declared other groups as undeserving of rights guaranteed in the Declaration of Independence and the Bill of Rights. It is hard to understand why the majority of African Americans continue to be loyal to a political party that overwhelmingly supports abortion. A court that can reinterpret the constitution at will can snatch freedom from any group it deems unworthy. Without a firm commitment to liberty for all, there may come a time when there will be liberty for none.

A secular education that has abandoned truth produces a philosophical foundation that cannot sustain freedom. Former Communist, Whittaker Chambers said, "What I sensed without being able to phrase it was what has since been phrased with the simplicity of an axiom: 'man cannot organize the world for himself without God; without God man can only organize the world against man.'" (12)

It is imperative that Americans recognize the connection between truth and liberty if the freedoms we have enjoyed are to continue to be the heritage of our children and grandchildren. However, for this to be accomplished, there has to be a consensus about what constitutes truth and about its source. Currently there is much confusion about this issue even among those who call themselves Christian.

Surely the beginning point to a consensus on truth is the public recognition that there is a source for establishing the difference between good and evil. If "good" exists there must be criteria established by a source higher than ourselves. Truth can only exist if it conforms to a standard. That standard has to be God. America and the world can only hope to experience liberty when they acknowledge that there is a God and that He is a God of goodness and righteousness. Such a God is concerned about justice, fairness, benevolence, and love. Whittaker Chambers summed it up quite well when he said, "God alone is the inciter and guarantor of freedom. Religion and freedom are indivisible. Without freedom the soul dies. Without the soul there is no justification for freedom." (13)

Francis A. Schaeffer in *A Christian Manifesto* claimed that "The law, and especially the courts, is the vehicle to force (a) total humanistic way of thinking upon the entire population." (14) Schaeffer saw a dangerous threat that could take place in western societies due to a collapse of civility and the ensuing chaos. He believed that no society could continue under the type of "form-freedom" democracy that America enjoyed for the first two centuries if the religious basis for that democracy crumbled. Instead there would inevitably arise an elite to rule from a type of tyranny. He saw the Supreme Court as possibly becoming that elite. His reasons were: the tendency of the court to rule on the basis of arbitrary law, the current practice of legislating from the bench, and the court's increasing power over the other two branches of government.

Schaeffer claimed that Americans have forgotten that we have had such tremendous freedoms without leading to chaos because our government owed its very existence to a Judeo-Christian consensus with its high view of life and the form-freedom balance on which it was built. He believed that none of these is natural in the world but "based on the fact that the consensus in the beginning of our democracy was the biblical consensus." (15) Schaeffer saw an open window of opportunity for Christians to sound the alarm and to take political action. He believed that there was a new wind blowing in the 1980s toward conservatism and a return to morality. However, his warning was that "this does not mean the new wind will automatically keep blowing. It does not mean we can return to the practice of false views of morality. And it does not mean we can withdraw from a struggle for continued reformation." (16)

"See to it that no one takes you captive through hollow and deceptive philosophy, which depends on human tradition and the basic principles of this world rather than on Christ."

(Colossians 2:8)

PHILOSOPHY AND THE TEST FOR TRUTH

Was God holding out on Adam and Eve?

"What is truth?" (John 18:38) Jesus was asked this question by Pontius Pilate. Jesus had just stated, "I came into the world to testify to the truth. Everyone on the side of truth listens to me" (John 18:37). In John 14:6 he said, "I am the way and the truth and the life." These words assure us that eternal truth cannot be separated from the person of Jesus Christ.

Every philosophy must begin with some assumption about God and about the issue of truth.

The secular philosophy, the one being caught as much as taught in America's public classrooms, says that we, individually, must determine what is right and what is true. The secular world teaches that truth changes with every generation, but Hebrews 13:8 states that Jesus Christ (who is the embodiment of truth) is "the same yesterday, and today, and forever," and Malachi 3:6 says, "I the Lord do not change." Jesus made it clear that his words would "never pass away" (Matthew 24:35).

Even scientists who reject creationism recognize that the universe is not eternal, that it is running down and at some point in time, it will end. Though their own scientific "evidence" points to a specific beginning of time and space (the big bang), they cannot conceive of anything outside of nature before the beginning or after the end of the universe. In fact, they categorically deny the possibility.

The apostle Paul in the book of Romans said that the creation of the visible world itself shows the invisible qualities of God. He stated further that even though people could know something about God through what He has made, the wicked refuse to give him thanks. They allow their thinking to become futile, and proclaiming their own wisdom they become fools.

The Bible describes a fool as someone who despises wisdom and discipline (Proverbs 1:7), and who finds pleasure in evil conduct (Proverbs 10:23). It declares that fools mock at making amends for sin (Proverbs 14:9), and they die for lack of judgment (Proverbs 10:21). In Ecclesiastes the writer says, "The heart of the wise is in the house of mourning, but the heart of fools is in the house of pleasure" (Ecclesiastes 7:4). Paul admonishes Christians to "not be foolish, but understand what the Lord's will is" (Ephesians 5:17). Proverbs tells us that the knowledge one needs to have begins with the fear of the Lord (Proverbs 1:7). The Bible teaches that the wise seek out the truth by looking to God and his Word, but those who scorn the wisdom that comes only from the Lord are fools, and their foolishness will destroy them.

Though there have been attempts throughout recorded history to do away with the Bible, it has endured. Governments and people who have tried to eradicate the

Bible have faded away themselves, but the Word of God still stands.

In the beginning of this nation, America's schools taught respect for the Bible and its teachings. Several of our major universities were founded to train people in the truths of God's Word. However, in recent times, those teachings have been barred from public education, and even many Christians have bought the idea that education and religion not only can be but must be separate. Our public schools are now incapable of teaching truth because the progressive philosophy behind public education denies the existence of such.

Humanist educators embraced the progressive label much the way homosexuals usurped the more likeable sounding word "gay." Progressive had the ring of moving forward, making progress, evolving upwards, and its mere use would draw a favorable response. Nowhere in the label was there even a hint of the philosophy's origin.

Much of the progressive philosophy on education, science, and religion came from nineteenth century philosophers such as Kierkegaard. Their philosophy denied that religious truth is rational. Kierkegaard wrote several books to show that faith is absurd and that true belief can be measured by the degree to which one is willing to abandon himself to it in spite of its absurdity. In other words, he denied that there is any objective, rational, and ever-lasting truth. These teachings have greatly influenced existential thinking and are closely akin to what is believed by many modern theologians in our universities. They have accepted the science of naturalism and materialism and have relegated religion to whatever warm, fuzzy feeling people want to assign it. They have given credence to the modern thought that each person must discover his own truth. In doing so they must deny the deity of Christ, his resurrection, and his right to rule the earth, as the Bible says he certainly will when he returns to it physically.

Existentialist philosophers denied that there is any law of nature that is universal. Such a law would be one that would allow all cultures to recognize certain behaviors as wrong. C. S. Lewis, in his book *Mere Christianity,* said that "human beings all over the earth have this curious idea that they ought to behave in a certain way, and cannot really get rid of it." (1) He goes on to say that a second universal phenomenon is that "they do not in fact behave in that way." (2) After studying and comparing the moral teachings of different ancient civilizations, Lewis was struck by how much alike they were to each other and to our own culture. Their sense of right and wrong and fair play seemed to point to a "law of nature" that people understood without having to be taught.

However, all people everywhere will make excuses for their failure to behave in the way that they expect others to behave toward them. Mankind is capable of developing whole philosophies to excuse wrong behavior, but in the depths of their souls there is a knowledge of their own imperfection. The Bible describes what happens to such people. It says,

> Since they did not think it worthwhile to retain the knowledge of God, he gave them over to a depraved

mind, to do what ought not to be done. They have become filled with every kind of wickedness, evil, greed and depravity. They are full of envy, murder, strife, deceit and malice. They are gossips, slanderers, God-haters, insolent, arrogant and boastful; they invent ways of doing evil; they disobey their parents; they are senseless, faithless, heartless, ruthless. Although they know God's righteous decree that those who do such things deserve death, they not only continue to do these very things but also approve of those who practice them.

Romans 1:28–32

We have seen the escalation of wrong behaviors throughout American culture, and we have even seen how some in our government and leaders in education have condoned such behaviors. It is no wonder that we are dealing with lawlessness in the land as never before in our history. When a society refuses to recognize the truth of the fallen nature of mankind, it will not and cannot restrain it.

There was a time when civilized societies recognized a direct link between education and the search for truth. The book of John in the Bible starts with a description of the beginning of all things in the universe. God spoke order into the cosmos. True science and true mathematics are based on immutable laws put into place by the Creator. Scientists can only find out about the universe because those laws are there, and because they don't change. Many of the greatest scientific advancements have come through the hands and minds of Christians because they expected to discover orderly truths in nature. However, modern education teaches that everything in existence came about as mere chance. Once the material energy chance view of life is espoused, everything else is up for grabs.

Post-modern America has come to believe that only that which is scientifically verifiable can be considered "true," even though scientific verification is not possible without the orderly and unchanging laws at work in the universe. Perhaps for that reason, most Americans still say that they believe in God. Ironically, however, according to pollster George Barna, less than twenty-five percent of Americans believe in absolute truth. What this seems to mean is that Americans are very confused about who God is and about who we are.

During the summer of 1998, a conference was held in Berkeley, California, to which scientists of any faith were invited to offer ideas about how religion and science could come to some kind of agreement. The conference was promoted and funded by the Templeton Foundation, a philanthropic organization that grants large sums of money to religious people who make worthy contributions to society. Many of the guests may have been sincere believers and outstanding in their scientific fields. However, all that appeared to be accomplished was that some speakers admitted they believed in God because of the order of the universe. There was an apparent consensus that for the time being science and religion are incompatible and must go their own separate ways, because only science is verifiable, while the existence of God is not and must be left in the realm of the unknowable. (3) Therefore, science (naturalistic science, which denies a Creator) can be allowed in schools, but religion can't. Who could argue that the education deck is stacked against any search for truth?

Many Christians believe that scientific means can be used to determine the reliability of the Bible, and much evidence has been gathered. Many manuscripts have been discovered and analyzed. Archaeology has confirmed much of biblical history. The Bible was written by at least forty different people living hundreds of years apart. It is surely an impossibility for a book written by such diverse writers over such a large span of time to be so compatible throughout and to be so without provable error. Groups of self-proclaimed scholars such as the "Jesus Seminar" have tried to discredit the Bible, but they have only succeeded in discrediting themselves. Other reputable scholars have taken issue with them and have presented a great deal of evidence for the truth and accuracy of the Bible. Even some agnostics who have taken a close and unbiased look at the evidence have discovered that Christianity offers more complete answers to age old questions than does any other worldview. The answers are far more rational than those offered by naturalism because one only needs to look at the incredible order and beauty in the universe to see that creation makes more sense than a great cosmic accident. It has been said that it takes much more faith to believe in evolution than in creation.

If God is true and the Bible is his revealed Word, it is for all people and for every part of their lives, throughout all ages. It cannot be both true and at the same time be irrelevant to science, education, politics, sociology, law, or any other issue.

Those of us who believe in absolute truth as revealed in the Bible must take a stand. We must let our voices be heard in the public square. We can not allow secularists to muzzle us and deny us the freedom to participate in our democracy. Furthermore, we have to realize that any education that denies truth is bogus. It is not something we should want for our children. It must be underscored that we cannot separate education from philosophy. We cannot separate educational philosophy from the issue of truth. We must keep in mind that every philosophy is based on a worldview, and every worldview makes certain assumptions about reality and specifically about truth. Anyone who denies this is either ignorant or devious.

Former atheist, Lee Strobel, attempted to use his journalistic investigative talents to prove Christianity a hoax. In his book *The Case For Christ*, Strobel describes how the evidence was so overwhelmingly in favor of the biblical Jesus, that he became a believer. He quoted one expert source as saying, "We have better historical documentation for Jesus than for the founder of any other ancient religion." (4) He went on to say, "The appearances of Jesus (after his death and resurrection) are as well authenticated as anything in antiquity." (5)

Unlike the Bible, many scientific theories have ultimately proven to be mistaken. Paul Little reported in his book *Know Why You Believe* about a brochure published by the French Academy of Science in 1861. It was a compilation of what Little called "fifty-one so-called scientific facts that controvert the Word of God." (6) Mr. Little pointed out that not a single one of those "facts" is accepted by scientists today. Not one! It has been said that yesterday's science texts read a bit like today's comic books.

Although there is evidence for micro-evolution within species, the larger theory of evolution is not verifiable because it cannot be observed or tested, and there were no eyewitnesses. The fossil record does not support it. New advances in DNA research confirm that the kind of changes in genes called for in Darwin's theory would have been lethal and couldn't possibly have advanced life. Darwinian evolution is losing credibility among many evolutionists, and they are searching for new explanations and supports for their belief in materialistic naturalism. Many credible scientists, such as embryologist Jonathan Wells, have pointed out major deceptions about evolution that appear in leading American textbooks. Every biology student needs to hear about these.

An educational system which ignores or denies truth is an illegitimate system, and its philosophies will at some point clash with reality. It will ultimately fail the test. A good objective look at what has happened to education in America will bear this out.

Surveys have continued to show a decline in adult literacy in America over the past twenty years. Statistics now show that close to forty percent of all Americans are functionally illiterate, meaning they cannot read a work application or write a few simple sentences to describe themselves.

Even those who are willing to use every spin tactic known to man to prove America's schools are not failing to educate, must admit things are not good. The National Assessment of Education Progress (NAEP) has been used since 1971 to determine how well U.S. students are progressing. Comparisons over the last thirty years have shown no significant improvement, despite spending increases that boggle the mind. In 1994 it was found that forty percent of students being tested scored below what is considered the "basic" level on the test. By the turn of the millennium, NAEP statistics showed closer to fifty percent below the "basic" level in reading. Although some progress has been evidenced since the "No Child Left Behind" policy of President Bush, American education still has a long way to go. Education researchers complain that the criteria set for the levels of achievement are arbitrary and don't take into account all the factors that influence student performance. However, these same people don't have much to say about the fact that more and more students have been either eliminated from taking accountability tests or have been given extra help because of "learning problems." Some estimates place the percentage of American students now being labeled as "learning disabled" at close to twenty percent. It is a fact that in some districts, even the reading portion of the state tests is read to such students by teachers. In some districts all students are allowed to use calculators on math tests, and some questions involving measurement provide information once thought to be basic, such as how many ounces there are in a pound.

Certainly we need to ask the question, "Why are America's schools failing to teach children to read and write?" There have been endless debates on this question. Most of them focus on reading methods, particularly on phonics versus whole language. Both sides haul out statistics to prove their method is superior. Particularly impressive among those is the case with California. California was one of the leaders in the nation in switching reading instruction in the early grades to whole language methodology. In 1992 the state ranked thirty-eighth on its NAEP scores and fell to dead last by 1994. After mandating a return to phonics instruction, California's scores improved. Sacramento boasted a jump of fifteen points on second grade scores in 1999. As impressive as this is, this writer believes the root of the problem goes deeper. Could it be that some of those at the top of the education hierarchy want to manipulate what is taught to children in order to keep control over what they believe and how capable they might become of seeking out truth for themselves? Is it possible that the powers behind the education hierarchy want to produce a citizenry that can read well enough to receive the desired propaganda but not well enough to pursue the truth?

Since the beginning of public schools in the United States there has been an ongoing debate, a clashing of philosophies, a struggle of ideologies. As already discussed, the first question that must be answered is what purpose does education serve. Other important questions include: What are legitimate responsibilities of the schools? What constitutes a good education? What are the best ways to teach? Is the same education appropriate for all children?

There have been two major viewpoints from which answers to these questions have been offered. They have often been referred to as the "traditional" and the "progressive." It can be difficult at times to separate the two since the goals occasionally overlap and similar terminology may be used.

For this reason discussions about educational theory can create a great deal of confusion for parents and teachers alike. However, if one hopes to understand where American education has been and where it is going, it is imperative to recognize and separate the philosophies behind these two competing viewpoints. Although the lines separating them may seem to be a little blurry at times, nearly all of education practice falls under one or the other philosophy.

It is possible to get a better perspective if you compare the two theories to the construction of a building. Two buildings may use some of the same materials and similar workmanship in the construction, but it is the foundation that will determine the ultimate strength of the building. For that reason this discussion will focus mainly on the foundations of two philosophies, and it will touch on how these affect the curriculum, teaching methods, and assessment.

The traditional education philosophy says that the purpose of education is to enable individuals to acquire knowledge and skill in order to prepare for work, to make life's decisions, and to be better citizens. In America, early attempts to educate were meant to provide literacy so that every person could read the Bible and apply its truths to his or her own life.

Traditional education stressed the teaching of specific subjects such as reading, writing, arithmetic, geography, history, and grammar. Patriotism was considered important, and civics lessons focused a good deal of attention on the superiority of American democracy over other forms of government. In the early grades, education was the same for all students, but beginning in high school, some students pursued more challenging academic material in preparation for college, while others took general education courses or some type of vocational training.

Under the traditional philosophy, development of character, and spiritual growth followed the dictates of the home and the church. The schools taught the importance of morality and gave respect to the contribution of religion to our society. Children were taught to respect their parents, teachers, and other authorities. It was common for teachers to refer to the Bible, to have children pray at some point in the day, and to invite Christian leaders to invoke God's blessing on school activities.

The progressive viewpoint, reaching prominence under John Dewey in the early part of the twentieth century, saw education as the means to the creation of a socialist society. It was to be the vehicle by which all of our moral and social problems could be solved. It had less to do with the acquisition of knowledge and specific skills, and more to do with the development of appropriate attitudes and social behaviors. It is important to remember that Dewey and his associates adopted the naturalist view that the cosmos was supreme, that everything evolved from matter solely by chance, and that man was just a more highly evolved animal and without a soul.

John Dewey stated, "I believe the social life of the child is the basis of concentration or correlation in all his training or growth. I believe therefore that the true center of correlation on the school subjects is not science, nor literature, nor history, nor geography, but the child's social activities." (7)

Dewey's educational philosophy was heavily influenced by the works of psychologists and philosophers such as William James, Sigmund Freud and Karl Marx, as well as by Charles Darwin. His ideas also seem to reflect those of the eighteenth century French philosopher, Rousseau, who believed that society must be reorganized into communities in which all persons' behavior could be controlled, desires limited, and all energies directed toward total involvement in community life.

In 1933 Dewey and thirty-three others signed the Humanist Manifesto. In this they made it clear that they saw their brand of education as the savior of society. The Humanist Manifesto II stated "No Deity will save us: we must save ourselves." (8) Humanists went on to say that "ethics is autonomous and situational, needing no theological or ideological sanction." (9)

In 1918 the National Education Association had, under Dewey's leadership, drafted the following list of cardinal principles for schools:

1. Health

2. Command of Fundamental Processes

3. Worthy Home Membership

4. Vocation

5. Citizenship

6. Worthy Use of Leisure Time

7. Ethical Character

Of these goals only the second one could be considered

strictly academic. Obviously John Dewey and his colleagues did not think that any area of a child's development ought to be left to the home and the church. Followers of Dewey have attempted throughout the years to increase the role of the public schools in the raising of children, with disastrous effects on academic achievement and society as a whole.

To their credit, these educators recognized the importance of building ethical character. However, it must remembered that they had already rejected God, so on what were their ethics to be based? Since Dewey and other humanists believed man to be his own god, the philosophy of situational ethics was born. Man from his own heart would determine right and wrong according to the situation.

Dewey's counterparts have been at war with traditionalists over the years. They have been determined to gain control over American society through the vehicle of public education in order to create the perfect society they envision. In their minds, humanistic education is all that is needed to solve all human problems. A bumper sticker put out by the Missouri State Teachers' Association a few years ago reflected this. It stated that *"Teachers are the solution."* Dewey himself said in his essay "My Pedagogic Creed," "I believe...the teacher always is the prophet of the true God and the usherer in of the kingdom of God." (10) One must keep in mind here that Dewey signed the Humanist Manifesto, which stated clearly the humanists' rejection of a supernatural creator God who is sovereign over mankind. They believed man totally evolved from forces of nature and does not have a soul or supernatural spirit. Their philosophy, the humanist religion, has become the foundation of public school education, and its aim is to remake society so that it conforms to their ideals.

In order to obtain the control they believe is needed, public education leaders, especially political leaders in charge of education associations, will spare no effort to either remove or gain more control over private education. Particularly troubling to them are parochial schools, which they see as the biggest threat to their goals. Every public teacher's education association has stated its objection to vouchers and school choice initiatives that include private or parochial schools. They have so successfully manipulated the press and the political climate that choice in education is considered a threat by a possible majority of middle class and wealthier Americans. One of the most politically charged words used today is vouchers. The establishment has succeeded in evoking such negative reaction to the term that it is difficult if not impossible to get accurate polls on whether or not a majority of Americans would like to be able to decide for themselves how and where to educate their children. Taking a stand for choice in education today is politically incorrect, and politicians who do so may very well seal their downfall.

Much of the controversy over education revolves around the question, "what is the school's responsibility?" It once was easy to say the school's responsibility is to teach children what they need to know. That has all changed. Today the very word "teach" has gotten a bad name among the more "enlightened" educators who are driving the reforms. They prefer the word "facilitator." Teaching, they say, puts the emphasis in the wrong place. Teaching implies transfer of knowledge from the head of the teacher to the head of the child, and they believe this is faulty pedagogy. They don't believe that children need such knowledge. What the reformers believe children need is guidance toward higher levels of thinking, where they will be able to use knowledge instead of spending so much time attempting to acquire it. Today's education experts believe in teaching *how* to think (critical thinking) and not *what* to think (knowledge).

The dictionary defines the word teach as: "to impart knowledge by lessons, give instruction to, to communicate the knowledge of; to train by practice or exercise." (11) The word knowledge means: "a result or product of knowing, information or understanding acquired through experience." (12) The word "facilitator," which the reformers prefer over teacher, comes from the French word facile which means requiring little effort. The word facilitate means to make easier or more convenient.

In spite of all the talk about higher standards, there is no doubt that our education system has worked overtime to make everything easier and more convenient. Even the Scholastic Aptitude Test has been scaled down to make it easier. This has been accomplished by allowing extra time, use of electronic calculators, fewer questions, requiring definitions only from context in reading, and dropping the most difficult linguistic portion of the test. Despite all these efforts to facilitate, the number of students scoring above 700 on the SAT declined from two and three- tenths percent in 1966 to one and two-tenths percent in 1995.

A look at literature from the reformers makes it obvious that they all seem to have a particular distaste for memorization and rote learning of such things as math tables, vocabulary, and spelling as well as facts from history and science. In Kentucky, reform leaders attempted to do away with local and state spelling bees altogether. This raised such a furor of criticism that they hastily tried to retreat.

Reformers do not want primary level students to spend time on learning the names and sounds of letters in preparation for reading. The theory is that you build a child's interest and self-esteem by allowing him or her to "read" right from the beginning, and then, if you must, you can slip in a little phonics later. They don't want elementary grade children to "waste" time learning math facts. Instead they say children should be taught more challenging subjects like algebra, geometry, and physics as early as sixth grade. Never mind the fact that in recent years schools have not been able to teach the basics of math successfully.

The reform philosophy says that children are naturally able to become "higher order" thinkers without having to spend time on the lower levels of knowledge, understanding, and application. In other words, kids aren't learning the basics because that is not challenging enough.

Does it not seem a bit strange that the same people who would have us believe it took millions of years for even the simplest life forms to evolve on earth, expect us to believe that children should learn in giant leaps without having to go through a series of smaller steps building progressively upon each other? We would do well to remember the verse in Hosea that says, "my people are destroyed for lack of knowledge." Knowledge has gotten a bad name with recent education reforms, and the destruction that goes with this abandonment of knowledge is becoming more apparent.

There is little doubt that literacy in this country has been on the decline for many years. Not only are children having more trouble learning to read, they are less able than ever before to learn by listening. Educators are told that lecture is one of the least effective ways to teach, even though for thousands of years oral tradition was the only way to pass on knowledge. One of the first things accomplished under reforms in Kentucky was to throw out textbooks from primary classrooms. This was presumably to keep teachers from using the old methods, which included lecture, thereby forcing them to find more creative methods to facilitate learning.

If the spoken word and the written word are no longer the primary tools for teaching, then what is? Teachers are reminded over and over again that children learn by doing, but it doesn't take a rocket scientist to figure out that not everything can be taught that way. What is actually happening is that children are being taught more and more by visual images. Not only do they spend hundreds of hours watching television and videos at home, they now encounter these regularly as part of their education. Most classrooms are equipped with televisions and DVD/VCRs, as well as one or more computers. No doubt these can be valuable tools for learning. However, when they become the primary source, a problem arises.

Noted expert on Christian apologetics (or reasoning), Ravi Zacharias, says that the further our generation gets away from the ability to learn through the oral and printed word, the more our capacity for abstract reasoning diminishes. He says that when you try to persuade most people through a logical progression of inductive reasoning, you will lose them half way through because their capacity for such has been "humiliated" through an excessive reliance on images. So, while our schools are calling for children to learn how to reason, they may be systematically helping to rob them of that which enhances such ability.

It is important for Christians to look at the words "knowledge" and "wisdom" as they are used in the Bible. The word knowledge is first used in Genesis 2:9, when God made to grow out of the ground the tree of knowledge of good and evil, and in verse 17 when he forbade Adam and Eve to eat of that tree. The serpent tempted Eve by telling her that if she ate the forbidden fruit she would become as a god—knowing good and evil (Genesis 3:5). Desiring to be wise (apart from God), she took the fruit and gave some to Adam as well. The question which comes most naturally to the mind of the critical thinker is, Was God holding out on Adam and Eve? Did he purpose to leave them in ignorance in order to prevent them from having something worth having? This is precisely what the devil wanted Eve to think and to ask. It is also the same question he wants us to ask. The rest of the Bible shouts a resounding "no" to the question, for it shows over and over again God's willingness to give knowledge and wisdom to those who ask him (II Chronicles 1:10–12 and James 1:5). We are reminded that "...the Lord gives wisdom and from his mouth come knowledge and understanding" (Proverbs 2:6). Wisdom comes from God, and it includes the right use of knowledge.

It comes with a willingness to hear instruction and apply it. The problem is the original sin of humankind - the desire to obtain God's knowledge apart from him. Such foolishness only leads to self-destruction.

Proverbs 1:7 states, "The fear of the Lord is the beginning of knowledge, but fools despise wisdom and discipline." Proverbs 14:12 tells us, "there is a way which seems right to man, but in the end it leads to death." Failing to recognize that God is the source of truth and wisdom is foolishness. Such foolishness will inevitably lead to the conclusion that there is no God but ourselves. Psalms 14:1 says, "The fool says in his heart, 'there is no God.'" Our nation, especially as it relates to education has been saying for some time, "There is no God."

As humanism is the philosophical foundation of public education in America, evolution is the law of the classroom. Evolution, by definition, teaches survival of the fittest. In other words, all things are evolving upwards to higher and better order—including humankind. The theory implies that we are learning more, and the more education we have the more perfect we will become. All of our problems, says the humanist, can be solved through education, our vehicle of evolution.

Evolution says that the universe and all in it were not designed, but occurred without purpose. It says that life essentially evolved from non-life. Talk about foolishness! Scientists proved long ago that life from non-life never happens. Still evolutionists cling to the faith that it must have happened at least once. Although there is not a single point in evolutionary theory that is beyond debate among evolutionists themselves, evolution has been accepted as fact in most science textbooks used for public schools in America. Many Christians have complained that evolution teaches their children to reject God as relevant to science.

In 1981 a law was passed in Louisiana mandating that schools balance the teaching of evolution with something called "creation-science." The statute never was accomplished because it was contested, and a federal judge ruled it unconstitutional. In 1987 the Supreme Court agreed that the law would create an establishment of religion in the public schools and therefore was unconstitutional. In other words, the Supreme Court of the United States held that evolution was the only explanation of origins that could be presented in the public schools of America. One has to wonder if this twisted thinking by our judges was produced by their humanist indoctrination at the hands of our education system.

In the 1990s, the Kentucky legislature attempted to remove the word evolution from the state curriculum and replace it with "change over time." Science teachers and education leaders along with a liberal press cried, "heresy!" Their reason was that "evolution is an idea that is fundamental for all biology," and that "the (new) wording allows more wiggle room for teachers not to teach evolution or not to teach it rigorously." (13)

In the spring of 2000, People for the American Way, a liberal organization, released results from a study it commissioned. The study aimed at finding the pulse of America on the question of evolution versus creation, and specifically to the teaching of such in the public schools.

The poll involved 1500 people from different segments of American society. What they found was that eighty-three percent of those polled supported the teaching of evolution, and sixty-eight percent believed that the teaching of evolution did not contradict the belief that God created humans and guided their development. (14) However, an article in *The New York Times* about the study quoted Dr. David Haig, an evolutionary biologist at Harvard University. Dr. Haig said, "it is logically inconsistent both to believe in the theory of evolution that humans did descend from animals, and to believe the opposite, that they were created in their present form." (15) Dr. Haig put into words what most if not all evolutionary scientists believe, and that is that you cannot accept the thesis that all life evolved without design or purpose, purely from material energy and also believe that an intelligent designer directed it all. The Times article also quoted the chairman of the market research firm that did the study. He "suggested that the public's sense that creationism and evolution are compatible 'translates in a pluralistic society and public to there being a place for both.'" (16) What these findings really say is that there is now a great deal of confusion about the whole issue throughout the nation. When most Americans see no conflict between the two worldviews, the nation is in more trouble than we realize. The worldview we embrace colors every part of our society and affects not only our philosophies and beliefs, but all the ways in which we approach education.

Many ministers have come down on the side of evolution if not directly, at least indirectly. They object to the inclusion of the creation story in public classrooms and consider it a violation of church/state separation. They believe that the Bible is a pre-scientific document, and that it relates only to doctrine, not science. In other words, the Bible cannot be taken seriously in matters of science and understanding. They fear putting the Bible on the same intellectual footing as *The Origin of Species.* Some even appear to believe that anyone who accepts the Bible as the greatest written authority on truth is not only ignorant but a threat to democracy. Perhaps this sheds some light on the findings of pollster George Barna, that the majority of ministers in this country no longer hold a truly biblical worldview. One has to wonder why and where our church leaders lost the conviction that truth exists and that it comes from an almighty God.

Evolution's defenders don't understand why people of faith can't just recognize or accept the "fact of evolution" and separate it from their faith. The fact is that many Christians have tried to accept evolution and make their faith conform to it. What they seem unaware of or disinterested in is that evolutionists disagree among themselves on literally every point of evolution theory. The only thing they do agree upon is the presumption which they have falsely labeled "the fact of evolution." They can prove virtually nothing about how it occurred.

The problem with attempting to blend one's faith in creation with evolution is that inevitably the tenets of evolution will prove false. The fossil record referred to continually shows only sudden appearances and disappearances of species with no evidence of intermediate or transitional forms. Darwin himself was convinced that such missing links were crucial to his theory, and he was sure that they would eventually turn up with more complete fossil investigations of the future. Such has not been the case, so scientists have begun to seek other avenues to support their beliefs. They seem to have accepted evolution on faith and are sure that one day they will have the proof. What will happen to the faith of Christians who have conformed their beliefs to fit the theory of evolution when it becomes obvious that the proof is not there?

In his book *Darwin on Trial,* Phillip E. Johnson related a very interesting question asked in a lecture by Colin Patterson, senior paleontologist at the British Natural History Museum. He asked an audience of experts if any of them could tell him "anything you know about evolution, any one thing that is true?" Apparently no one could. Mr. Johnson says that when Mr. Patterson tried the same question on other groups of scientists, he was also met with silence—until finally one member ventured, "I do know one thing—it ought not to be taught in high school." (17) Why is it, then, that educators are so convinced that it must be taught in high school? There seems to be a gap between where the scientists are and where educators think they are. This may have something to do with the fact that teachers spend a great deal more time studying theory than actual science. For all their intellectualism, many educators are very poor critical thinkers themselves, preferring to grasp what comes to them from professors without question and then dutifully passing it on to their students.

Evolutionists are very dogmatic about what they believe, so much so that they are at times driven to name calling toward anyone who would disagree with them. They have been so successful at silencing criticism through intimidation that we have reached the current situation in public classrooms where the theory of evolution is the only discussion of origins permitted. So much for critical thinking!

Dr. David A. Noebel, in his book *Understanding the Times*, reminds us that "faith is critical in every philosophy" and "The individual developing a philosophy must be extremely careful to base his case on the most truthful assumptions - otherwise, should one of the assumptions be demonstrated to be untrue, the whole philosophy will crumble." (18) Dr. Noebel predicted that if and when evolution crumbles, "Marxism and Humanism are intellectually dead." (19) Since these philosophies underlie so much of what post-modern Americans believe, it is interesting indeed to consider what the impact would be if they were to go up in smoke.

The public school system in America bought into humanistic goals for education. Educators are now so busy trying to be all to all children that real teaching has taken a back seat. The system has denied or ignored the existence of truth. Instead of equipping students with tools for the pursuit of knowledge, educators have emphasized political correctness. The schools' attempt to create a new social order has failed to produce a caring and orderly citizenry. Instead it has seen the rise of a self-absorbed, cynical, and increasingly violent society.

Progressive education has failed, but there is little hope that our leaders will recognize the source of the failure and take any action to correct it. The rise of Christian schools, particularly those that have returned to successful teaching methods, is making a difference. If this trend continues, and a new generation of well-educated young people who know the truth take their places in leadership roles across the nation, perhaps there is still hope for America.

There is the danger, however, that Christian schools could follow in the steps of the great universities established in the nation to teach Christianity and truth. It is particularly important that Christian schools be led by and every classroom staffed by Christian men and women well-trained in the Bible and knowledgeable about the philosophies that have influenced the failures of public education. It is essential that every Christian educator respect the integrity of Scripture and recognize it as the record of truth handed down to us from the Source of all truth.

"I, wisdom, dwell together with prudence; I possess knowledge and discretion. Counsel and sound judgment are mine; I have understanding and power. By me kings reign and rulers make laws that are just."

(Proverbs 8:12, 14–15)

TRUTH OR CONSEQUENCES

Is education tied to the rise of rebellion, depression, suicide, and immorality in America's youth?

School reform efforts always begin with the question, "What do we want children to know and be able to do?" Obviously this question must be answered before one plans a curriculum. Usually the answer to the question does not come from parents and the whole of society. It is left up to the education gurus with a generous mixing in of politicians. In most cases what really happens is that these groups skim over the knowing portion of that question and focus their efforts on what children should do. Reformers add to the criteria the question "What should children be like?" Or in other words, "What do we want them to become?" This part of the question is a legitimate one if there is a genuine consensus about morality and citizenship among those represented. However, the outcomes that we see from the current public education establishment do not represent such a consensus and are very predictable if one knows the philosophies behind so-called progressive education.

The Bible tells us that "when a wise man is instructed,

he receives knowledge" (Proverbs 21:11). It also warns that when we "stop listening to instruction," we will, "stray from the words of knowledge" (Proverbs 19:27). Throughout the Bible, especially in the Proverbs, knowledge, understanding, and wisdom are held up as worthy of pursuit. However, among the goals of education in recent years, a different pursuit has taken the place of these. Knowledge and understanding as discussed in the previous chapter have been given a bad name.

Education reform efforts are constantly a national concern because of the dismal success record of America's schools in recent years. Some hot reform topics include: "education for a global society," "world-class standards," "authentic assessment," and "multiculturalism and diversity training." All of these and many more are part of a larger umbrella, the label for which keeps changing as parents learn more about the philosophies behind them. One of the eclectic terms used for these movements is "outcome-based education."

On the surface, outcome-based education means setting testable goals and then testing and re-teaching until the goals are obtained. In actuality it is far more than that. A major problem with outcome-based education is that it provides an even more efficient way for politically correct sentiments based on a false worldview to make their way into the curriculums of our schools. This is because it allows reformers to redefine education, to throw out old standards, and to determine new purposes for schooling.

One of the favorite topics within reform efforts is "critical thinking skills." Just what do educators mean by the term critical thinking? The literal meaning of the word critical is "given to fault-finding or severe judgments, exhibiting careful, precise judgments and evaluations, analytical." (1) Though they would never say so, humanist reformers in our education system want children to become critical of the church, their parents, the history of our nation, and all of our moral traditions.

The critical thinking idea is part of what educators refer to as higher order thinking skills, made popular in education circles through the publication of *Bloom's Taxonomy of Educational Objectives*. Published in 1956, this work by Benjamin Bloom and other researchers categorized educational objectives from simple to more complex. They considered knowledge to be the extreme lowest level of learning.

By knowledge these educators were referring to the recalling of specific information. Who, when, how, and where questions are in this category. "Who was the first president of the United States?" "When was the Declaration of Independence signed?" The next level up the pyramid was comprehension, or understanding. Being able to restate information in one's own words and giving examples would be considered in this level. Above comprehension is application, or using what has been learned in a new situation. "Now that you have learned the components of a good lesson plan, you will plan and teach a lesson to a group of primary age students" is an example of application.

The three highest levels of education, according to Bloom and others, are analysis, synthesis, and evaluation. Bloom illustrated the levels of education with a pyramid. While analysis, synthesis, and evaluation were at the top of the pyramid, they were built upon the lower levels of knowledge, comprehension (understanding), and application. In other words, everything was founded on the base of knowledge. However, many modern reformers believe that since the top levels are the most important, educators need to place their emphasis on those. In fact, some of them believe it is possible and commendable to ignore or by-pass the lower levels of learning.

The pragmatic, existential thinkers pushing the reforms believe that all children are capable of higher-order thinking and should be taught at the highest levels. These are the levels that require the student to see parts and relationships, to arrange the parts to create the whole, and to make judgments about the subject. An analytical question might be, "What part of this story could not have happened in real life?" An example of synthesis might be to write a different ending for the story. Evaluation (or judgment) might have you choose a character from the story whom you would most like to meet and tell why.

Since the last three levels of learning are considered of a much higher quality than knowledge and comprehension, they are the basic components of what the education establishment calls "critical thinking" or "higher order thinking." Decision making (judgment or evaluation) receives perhaps the major emphasis in outcome-based education reform models, though it is only the smallest point on the learning pyramid and rests upon all the other levels.

It seems that a serious problem with the type of assessment

called for under this method of educating is that a bright student can answer some questions considered analytical, synthetic, or judgmental without either knowledge or comprehension of the subject matter in some cases. In fact, test reviewers brought up this criticism of the assessments used in Kentucky, the first state to implement outcome-based education state-wide. Testing experts stated that it was possible to do well on some parts of the tests without ever having spent time in class.

Educators in the reform movements believe that one must employ open-ended responses in the process of testing higher level learning. By definition, open-ended means there must be no correct answers. All answers that employ correct thinking processes are equally correct, and reformers believe that correct thinking processes can be taught. A basic assumption of this type of education is that all students, without exception, are capable of it. Invariably outcome-based education models use these components.

Although most proponents of this philosophy would not say so, and some may not even realize it, the idea has been around a long time. It says that a child is born with knowledge and understanding (the lowest levels of learning.) It is only necessary to help him find it within himself and to call it forth. The Greek philosopher Plato believed that when the soul left the body it went to a state where it could learn the facts about all things or ideas in the universe. He believed that after a time the soul would be born into a new person, but would have only a dim recollection of all it had learned in the realm of the dead and would long to return to that more knowledgeable state of the soul.

In Kentucky a major premise of the education model for reform was that *all children* (*no exceptions*) are capable of learning at high levels (meaning they can become critical thinkers.) "All" includes the child whose IQ may be fifty or below. If carried to its logical conclusion, this would have to mean that every child, regardless of circumstances, has within him or her higher order thinking ability, an ability beyond knowledge and understanding. Obviously this idea is totally contradictory to the notion that all life evolved from a meaningless bit of protoplasm in some primordial sea. However, it is consistent with some religious beliefs, especially those involving reincarnation. At this point the real critical thinker ought to be asking if those movers and shakers in the field of public education really believe in evolution after all. Is it possible that evolution is just another tool intended to remove every Christian influence from the classroom in order to open the way for other spiritual influences?

While teaching children how to think and make judgments may be a worthy goal, what most parents and many educators don't realize is that the present emphasis on critical thinking and decision-making in education has its roots in the philosophy of existentialism. Existentialism teaches that there can be no absolute truth, no certain knowledge, no objective standards or rules to help make choices—that life is a series of decisions that individuals must make on their own, with no way of knowing which ones are right. They simply make decisions based on their own thinking and accept responsibility for the results.

This agrees very closely with what John Dewey and other pragmatist philosophers believed.

Existentialists believe that religion is simply a matter of human decision and must be made separately by each individual in the absence of conclusive evidence. Friedrich Nietzsche, an existentialist philosopher in the late 1800s, proclaimed that God is dead and argued that religion could no longer serve as the foundation for moral values. He believed that religion had served its purpose and that people now ought to "critically" examine all of their values and the sources of those values.

Many of the leaders in the public education movement in this country bought into such philosophies. John Dewey was an atheist, so one of his goals was to separate the education of children from anything Christian. Dewey and his fellow educators believed that the social behaviors, feelings, and attitudes of children could be trained in such a way as to establish a new world order. It would be accomplished through a perfected ability to think critically. In reality it is nothing more than manipulating the direction in which children think so it conforms to humanistic philosophy.

Philosophy itself has been defined as having two important aims. First, to enable a person to understand the universe in which he lives, and second to sharpen his ability to think (making him a critical thinker?). The word philosophy comes from two Greek words: *philo,* meaning love, and *sophia,* the name for the goddess of wisdom. So philosophy would appear to mean the love of wisdom.

It is interesting to note that sophists were the group of philosophers who believed that anything one did to bring self-pleasure was okay as long as he could get away with it. To them, laws were only a means of keeping societal order, and as long as order was not disrupted, their actions had no consequences. They criticized morality and religion and described virtue as being successful in the world at getting your desires. (This should sound very familiar to us because it is highly representative of our culture.) The sophists went around Athens and neighboring cities advertising their wisdom and soliciting students from whom they were able to earn a good living. One could argue that these early philosophers were well on their way to becoming existential thinkers.

French existentialist philosopher Jean-Paul Sartre considered all of life meaningless and all human activity ultimately futile. It gives a pretty bleak and hopeless outlook on life. In fact, the only thing the existentialist can know for sure is, "I think, therefore I am." They insist that if an individual is to live meaningfully and "authentically" (a favorite term in outcome-based reforms) he or she must become fully aware of the true character of the human condition and bravely accept it. They believe that to learn how to do this one must study the most extreme kinds of human experience such as death, suicide, and all forms of alienation of the individual from others.

Most of us have heard of the practice in some schools in recent years of offering classes on death and dying. Students have been taken to mortuaries and even asked to touch a corpse. Young children have been asked to make caskets out of shoe boxes and to write their own obituaries. Critical thinkers need to ask why death education has become so popular, and what the real objective is.

Interestingly, existentialists believed philosophy to be more related to art than to science. Nietzsche seemed to almost worship art because he thought that it demonstrated a higher form of power than other forms of human endeavor, and to him the whole human condition was a journey to attain power over one's own passions. The marriage of art and philosophy becomes apparent when one examines carefully the curriculums that develop from the critical thinking movement in education. In the Kentucky model of outcome-based education, seven individual outcomes were devoted directly to Arts and Humanities, but art pervaded much of the rest of the curriculum in some form and was highly stressed at all levels.

In 1998 Kentucky's Daviess County Schools instituted a program designed to increase elementary school children's brain power, specifically the stimulation of neuron connections in order to improve their memory and problem solving skills. (2) The activities chosen for this instruction included regularly exposing them to the visual and performing arts, free piano or keyboard lessons, instruction in the game of chess and foreign language. These were to be a main focus in the elementary program, not just a frill, because it was seen as crucial to children's ability to learn at higher levels.

It is certainly not my intention to imply anything inherently evil about art or the study and enjoyment of it. God has gifted many individuals with wonderful artistic talents, and His own creation shows the greatest of all artistic genius. Music is considered the language of the soul, and it does appear to help children remember if their lessons are put to music. It is not my intention to discredit the idea that learning in the arts might enhance the brain's ability to function at higher levels. However, it is when the study and use of art are coupled with the idea that there are no limits—no right or wrong uses—that a problem arises.

Peter Kreeft, in his book *The Best Things in Life,* claimed that both Aristotle and Plato saw music as "more powerful than reason in the soul." (3) He quoted Plato as saying that "the decay of the ideal state would begin with a decay in music." (4) Most rational people would have to admit that we in America have seen a decay of massive proportions in some of the music in which our youth immerse themselves. In fact, many young people have admitted that their music led them to breaking the law in violent acts. Some of the music put out by rap artists displays the most disgusting disrespect for women imaginable. Can anyone reasonably doubt the role it has played in the increasing problem of rape? No doubt music has also played a part in pulling many children toward suicide.

Though in times past art imitated life, we have reached a time when more and more life imitates the images with which we have become inundated. Instead of enhancing our thinking, our reasoning ability has been subordinated. Reasoning expert, Ravi Zacharias, contends that excessive reliance on images robs people of the ability to think rationally. Those who supply these images through the movies, television, electronic games, and the Internet have trivialized everything to the point that anything goes, and there seems to be no concern at all for decency. Parents would be appalled if they knew the content of some of the videos shown in some junior highs and high schools. It was even reported that some teachers allowed their students to watch the awful beheading of an American at the hands of his terrorist captors via the Internet.

This idea that there are no right or wrong uses for art has also become apparent in relation to literature. Many parents have objected through the years to some of the reading material their children are exposed to through the schools. Though some may have over-reacted, there is plenty to be genuinely concerned about.

College students have been exposed to literature with depressing themes for some time. In past decades this tendency moved down to the high schools. I remember when the teenage daughter of a friend was having to write a report on the book *Catcher in the Rye* in the spring of her junior year. For those not familiar with it, this is a book about a foul-mouthed teenage boy, his mistrust toward adults, his sexual fantasies, and his fall into states of depression and thoughts of suicide. The book has no happy ending and no redeeming qualities. Just a few weeks after school was out that summer, the friend's daughter put a gun to her head and pulled the trigger, killing herself. Though there were most likely many factors at work, and she may have been depressed for some time; no one will ever know if the stuff she was forced to read added to her feelings of hopelessness.

Suicide, one of the leading causes of death among teenagers for some time, has now become a reality among grade school children as well. In the state of Maine, it was reported a few years ago that the suicide rate for children ages ten to fourteen had nearly doubled since the 1980s. (5) Perhaps there ought to be some studies done to see how much of an impact books with morbid themes and exposure to death and dying education have had on young children.

In July of 1998, a writer for the Associated Press described new books out for children that summer as "no light reading at the beach." (6) She went on to say that these books tackle tough subjects like the Japanese occupation of Korea, the military rule in Haiti, and the Serb siege of Sarajevo. The book that was the highlight of the article was one called *Out of the Dust,* a fiction set in the time of the American dust bowl. The newspaper writer described the book by saying, "no subject is too raw for this first-person tale, told in free verse: hunger, poverty, farm accidents, a mother's death, drunkenness, homelessness—all amid drought and sandstorms, shriveled crops and emaciated livestock." (7) The book's author noted in a draft of her acceptance speech for the Newberry Medal (an award given to top children's fiction writers) that "adult readers grimace at the events documented in *Out of the Dust.* They ask, 'How can this book be for young readers?' I ask, 'How can it not?'" (8) Children from grades four to eight were to be the target audience for the book. These same children watch hundreds, or more likely thousands, of violent acts on television, in movies and video games throughout their grade school years. Much of the music they listen to will have rebellious or morbid themes. Shouldn't reading, especially fiction, be a way for children to escape from the tragic realities of life to a more sane and wholesome plane, not a means for immersing themselves further into something that produces more anxiety?

In the summer of 2004, it was reported that a school system in Massachusetts had included on its summer reading list a book of "poems" written by gangster rapper, Tupac Shakur. A columnist reporting for the Fox News Channel who read the book said she had read better poetry on bathroom walls. In other words the book contained the same foul-mouthed, sexually explicit garbage as his "music." Tupac Shakur had been a drug dealing thug, arrested several times for sexual attacks on women and other misdemeanors before his death from a gunshot wound. The columnist reporting the story said that when teachers were asked to explain why they would encourage school kids to read such a book, officials said it was chosen because it would get kids to read. They appeared to have no concerns at all that it would send a message that such material has value and its contents sanctioned by authorities.

As has already been stated, the secular philosophy is the philosophy of our nation's public schools. It reached its prominence there on the back of the theory of evolution, which denied a Creator. A more accurate name for that philosophy is humanism. Humanism does not mean humane or humanitarian, which we ought to be. It means that man is the measure or the authority for all things and decides for himself what is true. It says that if there is a God, he is irrelevant, for mankind determines his own destiny and needs no intervention from any deity. It teaches that since there are many men (meaning all human kind), there are many authorities or truths. Therefore, truth is relative and cannot be absolute. According to this philosophy, God is only God as he exists in each person's mind—he is only what they make him to be. In other words, each person creates God in his own image. Therefore, all religions are equal. According to pollster George Barna, most Americans believe this to some degree. This includes church members and "believers." The question is, How did such nonsense become so widely accepted in our culture? The most obvious answer is, it took hold through the schools. It made its way from there into our newspapers, magazines, movies, music, politics, and, yes, even into religion.

Since schools cannot promote any religion other than humanism, certain effects are inevitable. A major effect is the loss of a value base, which results in chaos and insecurity. If we cannot teach that there is ultimate authority, we have no basis for right and wrong. If the here and now is all there is, and there are no ultimate consequences for actions except those imposed by other humans, the philosophy of sophism makes sense. Do whatever you can get away with. It is then every person for himself. This mindset leads ultimately to the rejection of all authority except that from within.

The seeds for our current condition have always been there, but most of what we are seeing now in the way of a morally confused society got its real grip on our country when the liberal thinkers began to insist on removing everything Christian from our schools. This led to the promotion and acceptance of a humanist worldview that is the complete antithesis to biblical morality. This all goes along with the notion that all children are capable of higher order thinking, meaning that they have within themselves the ability to make judgments about right and wrong. This ability is not to come from what they are taught by their parents or the church but from within, based on their own thinking.

The Bible says in Proverbs 29:18, "Where there is no revelation, the people cast off restraint, but blessed is he who keeps the law." Acceptance of the humanist philosophy and rejection of the Bible (God's revelation to man) led naturally to teaching sex education in the schools to children even in kindergarten. Those who believe that sex education in the schools was intended to keep children safe are living in a fantasy world. Sex education's intentions from the very beginning were based on supposed "findings" by self-proclaimed sex experts like Alfred Kinsey. Kinsey himself and many who worked with him were sexual perverts, some of whom were no doubt pedophiles. Their intentions were to legitimize their own behavior. Their ideas were given credence because they came through the university. In reality it all came down from the liberal academicians' acceptance of Darwinism and the resulting idea that there should be absolutely no restraints on sexual behavior. The biggest reason that liberals, especially those in academia, want to hang on to Darwinism in the schools is so that they can promote sexual license. Without evolution every other ideal of humanism would come crashing down.

The rise of homosexuality, pedophilia, pornography, abortion, and all kinds of sexual perversion to current levels has been a direct result of what has been passed off as educational enlightenment. In truth it has all been based on spurious research findings by people whose goal was to legitimize their own perversions. Humanists, however, cannot allow this to become public knowledge, because everything they stand for would then be in jeopardy.

Anyone who doubts that sex education in the schools has had a negative effect surely is not employing any kind of critical thinking. Those who believe that these "classes" are kept sterile and respectable need to think again. An acquaintance of mine who had just such a mindset took on the challenge of teaching such classes to elementary age children. Not long afterwards, she resigned because she had no control over the kinds of questions that could be asked, and it was her assigned responsibility to provide an answer to each one. Many of the questions were not intended to get legitimate answers to troubling questions. They were intended to shock, titillate, and amuse other students. The teacher said that most of the students asking the questions already knew way too much, and they were more than eager to pass it on to their classmates.

Middle schools, even in conservative Bible Belt areas, are dealing with students who try to find ways to have sex wherever they can find a place to be alone for a few minutes during the school day or after school hours while still at school. Teachers are warned that they should not send students out of class without supervision, not even to the restrooms. It has been estimated that as many as twenty-five percent of middle school students have experimented with oral sex, and some of those encounters have taken place at school.

We have reached a time in America where publicly there is very little knowledge about truth; there is no revelation (of God's laws) for most people. We cannot deny that our culture has cast off the restraints that once made us a decent society. The consequences have been disastrous. Lawlessness abounds. Children have been forced to surrender their innocence to a lewd, disrespectful, dangerous, self-indulged and warped humanity. The sanctity of marriage and home have been assaulted to the point of near death. The same perversions that brought down other civilizations are whacking away at us. Someone has said that if God doesn't do something about America, he may have to apologize to Sodom and Gomorrah.

Is there any hope left for America? Some would say no; we have gone too far and can not reverse the slide toward destruction. There are those, however, who still believe it is possible to turn the tide back. They realize that the only way possible is a revival even beyond the scope of The Great Awakenings in the past. Godly people across the nation need to be praying earnestly for such a revival. It is our only hope, other than the physical return of Jesus Christ as King.

"What has been will be again, what has been done will be done again; there is nothing new under the sun."

(Ecclesiastes 1:9)

TRUTH ABOUT CHANGE

Is there really anything new in education?

Change is inevitable, and nowhere is that more obvious than in education. Reflecting Solomon's words from Ecclesiastes 1:9, what seem to be "new ideas" in education almost always have been tried at some time in the past. Any teacher who has been in public education for more than ten years has seen educational practices come and go, and it is a virtual certainty that it is not the first time they have come and gone. This constant shift from "back to basics" to emphasis on "higher order thinking," from structure to open classrooms, from graded to un-graded, phonics to whole language, etc. is due to the struggle between the traditional and the progressive philosophies of education.

When I was an undergraduate in education in the late sixties, the latest fad was "discovery learning." The child was not to be told anything new, but allowed to discover the answers to his own questions; and those questions were to arise naturally out of a problem which the child had. The intention was to create an atmosphere where the child would have a need to know something and would then have to devise a means to find the answer—perhaps through experimenting or through reading selected materials. "Problem solving" were the buzz words, and grouping children together (cooperative learning) to do problem solving was the preferred way of going about it.

The only guest speaker I remember being invited to a college reading methods class was a young teacher who talked to the class about her innovative reading program. It was totally individualized, and her students read from children's literature books of their own choosing. There were no basal readers in her class (and surely no skills workbooks.) She kept "anecdotal records" on each child and had a "conference" with each one once or twice a week to determine needs and set goals (with the child's approval, of course.) She was confident that her students were making adequate progress, and assured the class that the parents were quite satisfied. That methods class did a couple of things to those studying to become school teachers. It left a bad taste in their mouths for the term basal readers. And, it convinced them that most of the teachers currently teaching just didn't know very much about proper methods; certainly not as much as they were going to be privileged to know. Current teaching ideas were hopelessly outdated, and theirs would be the future of education.

Even though that was over thirty years ago, that young lady could step right in to train teachers in the "new" methods of whole language instruction under the latest education reforms. Anyone familiar with what is going on in education in recent years will recognize that her methodology and even the terms used are essentially the same as those being taught to prospective teachers today and considered innovative and progressive. What this says is that teachers tried that methodology, found it unsuccessful, and returned to the tried and successful methods of the past.

One of my methods classes in college visited several modern schools around the university town. In a couple of these the walls had been taken down so that students in the primary grades could move freely from one location to another, or several classes could be grouped together in a central location. In one such school, children worked through programmed, self-checking materials at their own pace. It all sounded so modern; not at all like my school days. Children looked so happy and comfortable sitting or lying on the carpeted floors and seemed to be having lots of fun with an endless supply of materials and interesting things to do, as well as the freedom to choose their own activities. The class could hardly wait to get started. Their files filled up with ideas for enrichment, bulletin boards, crafts, games, and fun projects to do. They searched for books on enriching activities, but hardly gave a second thought to basic subject matter content. Basic skills just wasn't a very interesting topic, and was hardly ever mentioned in methods classes anyway.

When a parent asked during the my first teaching job why his child wasn't memorizing anything for history, the well-rehearsed answer learned from college classes was that children don't need to memorize facts. They just need to learn how and where to find information when and if they do need it. Besides schools were getting away from teaching history in the early grades and replacing it with social studies. This allowed more emphasis to be placed on studying the cultures of more modern societies, giving children a greater appreciation for diversity. More diverse heroes could be included in their studies, particularly those responsible for bringing about social change. However, by the mid-1970s, it was becoming painfully clear that students were not doing as well on standardized tests of achievement as they should. If those standardized tests had not been given, I would no doubt have been oblivious to the fact that students were falling behind on skills. After all, they were enjoying the classroom and had been successful according to expectations. Little by little, though, a shift was made that gave more time and attention to skills practice, and classes began to look more like those of the past.

The same call for a return to the basics was taking place across the nation. Apparently the falling scores on skills tests were having an impact on many classrooms. Maybe discovery learning was more fun, its impact dynamic, and results long-lasting, but perhaps it was not the most efficient method of teaching or appropriate for all learning. Perhaps an over-emphasis on it could even hinder some children from gaining essential skills.

I mistakenly thought the discovery method was a new innovation in teaching. However, more research showed that it was being pushed by the "progressives" in the 1940s and even earlier. My mother-in-law, a retired teacher, remembered visiting a university lab school in Terre Haute, Indiana, in the 1930s. The children in that primary class were studying trains. They had built a model of an engine out of a barrel and tin cans. Their reading, spelling, math, etc., all related to their train theme.

Under this method of teaching there is no set curriculum. The class designs its own curriculum according to the interests of the moment. It's easy to see that it would be most difficult to insure that all necessary skills were being covered in the order of progression needed across grade levels.

One of the first things elementary schools did under the reforms in Kentucky was to throw out curriculum guides along with all basal reading books so that teachers would be free to set their own goals. However, the state had set accountability guidelines that included rewards and sanctions. In other words, if the students did well, the teachers were rewarded with bonuses. On the other hand, if performance slipped, the state could take over the school and send in what they called "master teachers."

A friend of mine got a job teaching in a school that was under the tutelage of these education experts because of the school's low performance. He said that the teachers were being instructed in how to identify skills to be taught, write scope and sequence charts, and come up with a curriculum guide. Probably some of the older teachers realized that what they came up with had a strong resemblance to what they threw out ten years before.

If the universities had been trying to get teachers to teach with progressive methods since the 1930s, why hadn't it succeeded? Could it have failed for the same reasons in the thirties and forties as it did in the sixties and seventies? Was it because it hadn't been given a fair trial, or because teachers had been inadequately prepared? Or, was it possible that there was a basic flaw in the foundational premise?

I have come to believe that the heart of the controversy is not about successful methods for teaching children to read, write, and do arithmetic. After all, civilizations have been doing that for thousands of years. One would have to be extremely naive to believe that society couldn't develop a successful method for teaching children to read in three or four thousand years. All the confusion about what works and what doesn't work is merely a smokescreen to cover up the fact that what is at stake is political.

The Encyclopedia of Education Research acknowledged that "most studies have produced varied results" and that "research findings seem only to support a political agenda, not lead to improved practices." (1)

With public schools subject to a monstrous bureaucracy, and with billions of public tax dollars at stake, it is no wonder that there are so many federal and state programs vying for favor. These programs all mean jobs for people who have access to the most powerful union in America, the National Education Association; the very existence of which is to keep public dollars flowing into education jobs. Among the members of the organization are some men and women who have every intention of using their power to control the destiny of not only education in America but of America itself, and ultimately perhaps even beyond.

It should be no surprise that the NEA welcomes more government involvement in education. After all, the more the government is involved the more control the association will have over education philosophy and practice, as well as the flow of public funds into approved projects and programs.

"Education reform" is to a large degree just a euphemism for the National Education Association's attempts to gain more control, and it has been going on since the founding of the organization in 1870. However, efforts toward "reform" have accelerated in the past twenty-five years, thanks in part to the establishment of the Department of Education in Washington during the Carter Administration. It seems that just about everyone who holds public office wants to be identified with education reform. Supposedly the reason for this increased concern is the continuing failure of American schools to compete with other countries academically. Certainly it is true that America's academic performance has been in decline for several years, but have reform attempts really been designed to reverse that decline?

There has been a debate in academic circles for some years about whether America's attempt to educate the masses on an equal basis is part of the problem. After all, some other countries choose to educate only their most able students beyond a certain point. Children are sometimes separated into different schools on the basis of ability. And yet, reform attempts in America have tried to eliminate even the tracking of high school students into academic versus vocational concentrations. Reformers seem to object to special programs for gifted and talented students, claiming that such should be provided for all students, regardless of ability. Academic competitions in which only the best students participate are frowned on. Even grades, which indicate a form of competition to these people, are targeted for elimination.

One of the most controversial parts of the Kentucky

Education Reform Act was the mandating of the un-graded primary. Not only were students placed in multi-age classes, but they were no longer to be given grades for performance. They had no set curriculum, and memorization, drill, and other forms of objective learning were discouraged. In the first couple of years under the reforms, spelling bees were discouraged. After a large public outcry and much ridicule, backers of the reforms claimed they had never intended to discourage spelling bees. So, one has to wonder if academic superiority is after all the major goal of reforms, or is it something much more political in nature?

As has already been stated, even some education researchers admit that research in education is not always intended to improve practices but to serve a political purpose. A class in research methods is a required part of most master's degree programs for educators. One of the first things students learn in the class is that statistics can be used to "prove" anything you set out to prove, and the students in my college research class proceeded to do just that in their projects required for completion of the class.

Proverbs 18:17 says, "The first to present his case, seems right, till another comes forward and questions him." An important part of critical thinking surely is to listen to both sides of a controversy before making a judgment, especially one that will have long-lasting effects on many people. However, in the planning of education reforms, a narrow-minded approach usually wins out. In Kentucky, politicians and education gurus pushed their reforms through without any chance at close scrutiny from the public. They had their "research," and they were convinced, so they saw no reason to listen to any other side.

In the summer of 1998 a media firestorm occurred when CNN had to issue an apology for a story they had done supposedly documenting that a deadly nerve gas called sarin had been used by United States commandos to kill American defectors of the Viet Nam War in 1970. The two main producers of the report were fired following an investigation that showed there was no real proof to support their story. The attorney hired to investigate said in his review that, "the serious flaws stemmed from the journalists' deep belief in the story and the way they discounted contrary information." (2)

During that same time period "*The Cincinnati Inquirer* apologized and retracted its expose of Chiquita Brands International, Inc." (3) and paid the company ten million dollars to avoid a lawsuit. Syndicated columnist Clarence Page quoted Abe Peck, a former editor of the Chicago Seed, about the loss of the public's trust in the media. Peck said, "I never thought and still don't think you have to be objective to be accurate. You can have a tremendous point of view and still be accurate." (4) He went on to say, "The underground press got into trouble when we began to shape our news to fit our beliefs." (5)

For years the devastating results of tobacco were hidden because of supposed research that showed no link to cancer. It is seemingly impossible to get the truth about possible effects of the many additives and chemical changes in our foods. This should be a wake-up call to citizens that we can't always trust what we read in the news. We must be critical thinkers at all times.

Those who are familiar with the Scopes Monkey Trial will remember the Piltdown Man fossil now known to be a fraud and the pre-human fossil tooth from Nebraska Man later discovered to be from a pig. These "scientific proofs" were used to launch the theory of evolution into its present credibility in the classroom.

Educators, of all people, should know to examine research findings with a critical eye. Nevertheless, reformers in Kentucky determined in 1990 that the research on whole language was totally conclusive, enough so to mandate it for the entire state. This was taking place at about the same time that California was about to change back to a phonics approach after their experiment with whole language failed. Apparently, even though critical thinking was to be one of the main goals of the reforms, the framers of that legislation failed to use it themselves.

Readers not totally familiar with educational jargon may be wondering just what whole language is. The whole language philosophy is that children learn to read by reading and to write by writing; also that they learn to read by writing and to write by reading. What this means is that there are no prerequisite skills in order to read or write. It is somewhat like the theory that the best way to teach a non-swimmer to swim is to simply throw him into the water. The essence of the methodology is to so totally immerse the child in the printed word at a time when his brain is most adept at learning language skills that learning to read will occur naturally, almost automatically.

Whole language reading instruction focuses on reading books or stories to children until certain ones become so well known that the child can actually repeat the text from memory. "Big books" in which the text can be seen by all the children at once are placed on an easel, and the teacher uses a pointer under the words as he or she reads. Children are then encouraged to "read" the text with the teacher even though many of them would not be able to read any of the words in isolation, and, in fact, some of the children may not even know the alphabet yet. Another technique is to use "predictable books," in which the child can guess what will happen next and so be able to "read" it. This gives the child "a feeling of success" at reading. "Repetitive texts" supposedly facilitate the child's remembering the structure of whole words, making it unnecessary to recognize the parts. The teacher is not interested in whether the child can identify all of the words but in whether or not he is learning to enjoy reading and is able to reconstruct the message, using whatever cues he can such as pictures, predictability, and recollections of the story. This method is justified because it "makes reading meaningful, and puts the emphasis on understanding and enjoying a text rather than on decoding it (recognizing individual sounds and words.)" Again, the important thing is not what the child is learning but how he feels about it.

This all sounds reasonable and maybe even desirable. After all, who wouldn't rather be able to grasp something in its completed form without having to go through the tedium of building one small part of it upon another before reaching the goal. However, programs such as Project Read, a phonics based program out of Bloomington, Minnesota, authored by Victoria Greene and Mary Lee Enfield, Ph.D., have a great deal of research showing that many children can not learn by whole language methodology. Children with problems in perception, memory, or attention learn better through receiving direct, systematic, multi-sensory instruction. These children are not able to see a whole puzzle from its parts. The ability to immediately grasp the whole without having to manipulate the parts is determined by IQ and may also have a lot to do with right or left brain dominance. Those are not factors which teachers can affect to a large degree.

Whole language proponents remind us that all babies learn language by listening and imitating complete language forms—whole words and sentences. Certainly they are hearing complete language, but they learn to understand and to reproduce it in a very systematic bit-by-bit way. They learn to make individual sounds first, followed by syllables, finally by something closely resembling a real word, and then they begin to string words together by twos and threes to form simple sentences.

The "whole language" people believe that since the ultimate purpose of reading is to obtain meaning, then that is where we ought to start in teaching children how to read. While it is true that the ultimate goal of learning to read is to understand the meaning of the written words, as with any other skill there are many steps necessary to get there. The whole language theory when applied to music would say that since the ultimate goal of music lessons is to be able to produce music, then one would not spend time learning the notes nor practicing scales. They would simply listen, memorize, and imitate whole pieces of music. And, indeed, a few people can do that, but most cannot. (Even those who can do it usually admit that they are limited by not being able to read music and play it as it is written.)

So it is with learning to read. Individuals gifted in language seem to learn to read without effort. In most classrooms you will find some children like that. Others will find their own way of learning in spite of bad teaching methods. However, many children will not be able to learn to read unless they receive systematic instruction in fundamental skills. They will be labeled as either unmotivated or handicapped by low intelligence or a learning disability. Some of these children will become behavior problems in the classroom and may even be labeled as having emotional disabilities.

In 1998 a report out of Frankfort, Kentucky, showed a sixty-one percent increase over five years in the number of students needing special education. (6) Officials attributed the rise to better diagnosis at an earlier age, while admitting the number is still too low because many children with such disorders are never formally identified. What they failed to say was that at about the same time the reforms were instituted in Kentucky, a concerted effort was being enforced to make it much harder for teachers to refer students for testing for special education. Exaggerated paper work, meetings and other seemingly endless red tape led some classroom teachers to vow they would never refer another student. Despite those efforts the number of students needing help continued to rise.

In the first three years of the reforms, with attendance

staying nearly steady, the school where I taught went from one and one-half special education units to two and one-half units. At the same time, it also went from having one full-time Chapter I Reading teacher to two full-time teachers.

On a return visit to the school after a year away, I was appalled at the number of students in the primary classrooms who could not read. The classes were made up of Primary Three and Primary Four students (meaning second and third grade.) Some of these students had probably spent more than four years in the Primary program, since the state had mandated that students spend as much time as necessary in the primary in order to be ready for fourth grade before leaving the program. Two of the teachers shared their concerns that close to half of their classes were having serious trouble reading. One teacher made the statement that "these kids are non-readers," meaning they weren't just behind in their skills. They literally could read nothing on their own unless they had memorized it.

Nearly all educable children referred to special education programs in the lower elementary grades are children with reading problems. Most of those have average or above average intelligence and are classified as learning disabled. I had always suspected that many of those children could have learned to read if they had received direct, intensive and systematic phonics instruction in the beginning. However, by the time they were placed in special education many had given up, and all of them had learned bad reading habits, which are very difficult if not impossible to unlearn. Another factor against them is that their reading instruction time with the special education teacher is often limited. This is due to the fact that most of them by that time have to have help in all of their reading related subjects in order to keep up in the regular classes where they are "main-streamed" for a portion of the day.

The following is part of an actual referral of an eight-year-old child for special education services. It demonstrates the kinds of reading problems seen in children considered to be learning disabled. Of course a fictional name has been given to the child and information which could identify the child or his family has been deleted.

Background: Kent's primary block teacher is concerned about his reading, spelling and processing skills. Samples of Kent's written work reflect his difficulty with spelling. His written product after thirty minutes of creative writing time generally consists of a few illegible words on the page. When Kent is asked to copy from a book, he reverses, miscopies, and leaves out letters. Notes on Kent's reading provided by the Chapter One teacher indicate that Kent shows good comprehension, but poor decoding skills. Kent miscalls words as similarly looking words. He memorizes stories, but does not recall the words when they are presented in another context. Kent's classroom teacher and the Chapter One teacher noted that Kent has a good oral vocabulary and that he has intelligent responses to add to discussions. They note that Kent is enthusiastic and cooperative when he is provided with material at his reading level, which is about the 3rd pre-primer level. His classroom teacher noted that he is a good natured child. He has difficulty staying on task and most of his work is incomplete. Kent has not been retained.

Interventions: Kent has been receiving Chapter One services. The Chapter One teachers have worked with Kent individually and in a small group setting. Methods they have used to improve Kent's reading include: having him read with an eighth grader, reading passages to him before asking him to read, using predictable, repetitive stories, and using various learning activities to reinforce basic sight words. His classroom teacher has reduced the number of spelling words from fifteen to five, has him write his words three times every night for homework, and has had individual conferences with him about his reading. Kent has not made satisfactory progress with these modifications. He continues to have a small sight vocabulary and difficulty spelling correctly. Kent comprehends and remembers stories well, but he does not recognize the words he has learned in one story when the same words are presented in a different story. He can decode individual sounds, but does not apply decoding skills to reading stories.

It is most interesting to note that the methods used by the remedial teachers were the whole language methods which were already in use in the child's classroom. Although the description refers briefly to the fact that the child could "decode individual sounds" there is no indication that he was ever taught those sounds by his teachers, how to apply them, or even that there was a reason to apply them. In fact, whole language methodology discourages the use of decoding skills during the reading process based on the idea that it detracts from comprehension and enjoyment of reading. One can easily imagine what will happen after a few years if this child's special education teacher continues to employ this same methodology with the same failure to obtain positive results. The child's self-image will deteriorate, and his attitude toward school will certainly suffer as well. There is a very real danger that he will develop anti-social behaviors and become a trouble maker. He most likely will become a drop-out from school.

As a special education teacher, I was allowed a fair amount of freedom in choosing methods of teaching reading skills. A phonics-based program was chosen along with other methods. The phonics program used was systematic, intensive, and multi-sensory. It put everything to music and used charts and games to reinforce. Every student made progress with the program, usually more progress in one year than in the previous two to four years they had been in school. Not only did their reading improve but so did their spelling. It wasn't uncommon for regular classroom teachers to comment that in some ways these kids did better than their classmates.

My first class in a new Christian school had several students (nearly half) who had the same reading problems I had seen over several years in special education in public school. All of these children had spent three years already in public schools under the Kentucky education reforms known as KERA, and it was suspected that if they had remained there, several would have ended up in special education. Although a few of those students returned later to public schools because of difficulty keeping up with the rigorous academic curriculum, most were able to continue in the program and even to excel.

Subsequent classes, made up mostly of students who had been in the school for all or most of their schooling, had fewer and fewer children with reading problems. It must be noted, however, that when administration policy changed and new teachers were allowed to use the whole language methods, it appeared that the problems returned. During my last year in that school, a teacher shared that close to half of her students could not read on grade level. It surely was not coincidental that some of those students had primary teachers who preferred whole language instruction.

It has already been mentioned that in the whole language classroom writing is used to encourage and enable children to read. Much time is spent on "creative writing." The communication of ideas is the starting point for writing instruction rather than the ultimate goal. Children are encouraged to put their own thoughts on paper from the earliest days of instruction. These "compositions" need not contain any correct letters in the beginning or letters at all as long as the child can "read" his creation to someone else. The teacher may translate the writing for parents. The child may "read" the composition differently each time he is asked to share it, but this is considered unimportant since he is supposedly gaining an understanding of the purpose of writing. Gradually, through observing the teacher's writings and through her reading, the child will hopefully pick up cues which she will incorporate into her own writings. The teacher is to be positive and show respect for any attempt to write. It is believed by whole language proponents that this will provide encouragement, which will boost the child to continue writing, and improvement will follow naturally. Children are discouraged from being concerned with spelling in their initial efforts at composition.

One big problem with teaching writing this way is that beginning writers don't usually revise their writings. They are learning to be unconcerned about spelling (as well as punctuation and grammar), and it may be difficult to change this behavior once it is established. In a traditional writing class, the child who has gained a foundation for writing can then learn to use the writing process in generating his work. At that point he should understand that he will be rewriting a number of times, so it is not so important to be concerned about spelling in the initial phase of composition.

While memorization of books and stories is encouraged in whole language reading, memorization is discouraged in early mathematics instruction. The focus for math in the primary grades is on manipulation and experimentation. Problems must relate to the child's "real world," therefore numbers must represent something concrete with which the child is already acquainted.

"Box-It-Bag-It" and other manipulative type math programs involve collecting many different countable, measurable items. The items may then be used to demonstrate addition, subtraction, multiplication, and division, etc. as long as such represent real world problems. At this point beginning math students do not even need to know the names for the numbers, nor the symbols for them. Drill and practice are not considered appropriate for classroom instruction but can be a part of computer programs used by the students on a regular basis. Classroom time is considered to be too valuable to waste on memorization of facts. The emphasis again is on the *use* of numbers in problem solving activities.

Children move easily from the use of manipulatives in the primary grades to the use of calculators in the upper grades. Since the emphasis is on understanding the problem, concern for the child's skill in calculation is given low priority. Also, it is important to remember that all outcome-based models tend to focus on feelings rather than facts. The following is a humorous look at the changing methods for "Teaching Math":

Teaching Math in 1950

A logger sells a truckload of lumber for $100. His cost of production is 4/5 of the price: What is his profit?

Teaching Math in 1960

A logger sells a truckload of lumber for $100. His cost of production is 4/5 of the price, or $80. What is his profit?

Teaching Math in 1970

A logger exchanges a set "L" of lumber for a set "M" of money. The cardinality of set "M" is 100. Each element is worth one dollar. Make 100 dots representing the elements of the set "M." The set "C," the cost of production contains 20 fewer points than set "M." Represent the set "C" as a subset of set "M" and answer the following question: What is the cardinality of the set "P" for profits?

Teaching Math in 1980

A logger sells a truckload of lumber for $100. Her cost of production is $80 and her profit is $20. Your assignment. Underline the number 20.

Teaching Math in 1990

By cutting down beautiful forest trees, the logger makes $20. What do you think of this way of making a living?

Topic for class participation after answering the question: How did the forest birds and squirrels feel as the logger cut down the trees? There are no wrong answers.

Author Unknown

The discovery method is supposedly the theory behind the new math methods. Students do not spend time learning math rules or in practicing them for mastery. A friend of mine complained that his high-school daughter was having a very difficult time with algebra even after extensive tutoring. Her father attempted to help her and was surprised to find that the daughter had been given story problems but had not learned the basic algebraic rules that could be applied to solve the problems. He proceeded to teach her as he had been taught, and she was then able to use the rules to figure out the problems. When her teacher discovered what had happened, she called the father and insisted that he stop instructing his daughter this way because it was undermining what they were trying to teach her. The reasoning was that students will understand better and retain longer if they discover how to solve problems for themselves. As in any other area of education, some students will learn this way, but some cannot because their brains are not programmed that way. However, under reform efforts like those in Kentucky *every child* is expected to learn at high levels. The result has been that more students than ever have been flunking algebra.

So, in the end, what does work in education? For the teaching of reading, writing, and arithmetic, thoroughly tried and tested methods that have worked well for hundreds of years still yield the best results. However, those designers of such methods as whole language, discovery math, cooperative learning, and giving young students the responsibility for choosing and planning their own educations did not see a traditional education as their primary goal. Equipping students with the tools needed to pursue knowledge of the truth was never a part of the plan. The methods had to be changed in order to fulfill the new purpose of education, the creation of self-actualized human beings on the evolutionary path to a perfected society.

"For these commands are a lamp, this teaching is a light, and the corrections of discipline are the way to life."

(Proverbs 6:23)

TRUTH ABOUT OUR SHIFTING CULTURE

*Does education hold the power to change
the worldview of a nation?*

Much of the squabble in America has been about how much influence schools should have on the culture. Whether or not there is an agreement, schools do have power in shaping the culture. The biggest dilemma in the last century has been about what kind of culture we will embrace and who ought to make that decision.

Unfortunately we have allowed the universities and the politicians they produce to make the call. It is unfortunate because as Phillip E. Johnson, author of *Reason In The Balance,* noted, "If naturalistic thinking increasingly dominates public education at the primary and secondary levels, this triumph was possible only because similar thinking came to dominate the universities long before." (1)

Leaders in education began to embrace naturalism after an abandonment of the truth, which is in accord with objective reality. Phillip Johnson said that such an "abandonment of realism in morality is supposed to produce a kindlier, more tolerant society, but what it actually does produce is tribalism or partisanship." (2) Johnson stated that,

"There is a substantial literature suggesting not only that universities are in the midst of an intellectual crisis but also that campuses are centers of politicization and intolerance." (3) Who could argue that America is more divided than ever on cultural issues?

Author and frequent campus speaker, Ann Coulter is often attacked or attempted attacks are made on her because of her conservative messages. She says that when she offers the microphone to these oppositional students, they usually resort to making what they hope will be shocking statements about sex. According to Ms. Coulter, she seldom hears from a liberal-minded student who has thoughtful questions to ask or any credible argument to make. She attributes this to the fact that they have been spoon-fed the liberal dogma and never forced to think it through critically. They have bought into it hook, line, and sinker, and all they know is that they hate whoever doesn't agree.

There certainly has been a culture war going on in our society, but those who control education have had the upper hand because they also have a lot of control over the media and the courts whose philosophies the universities have produced. This has resulted in a constant bullying of the rest of society.

As already mentioned in the previous chapters, education leaders under John Dewey began to push for a greater role for the state in the raising of children. Dewey understood completely that the success of his version of utopia would only be possible through creating a new mentality, a new psychological attitude—a new culture. Hence, he wanted education to focus more on the social training, attitudes, feelings, and behaviors of children and less on teaching knowledge and skills. He understood also that there would have to be a breakdown of the traditional family if the schools were to create individuals with allegiance to the state as provider.

Under the Dewey version of utopia, the state would determine what constitutes morality. There began to be a push for more strict separation of the schools from religious influence. More emphasis was placed on teaching evolution in public schools in order to shift the established religion to scientific naturalism. Schools began to buy into the psychological theories of people like B. F. Skinner, Ivan Pavlov, and Sigmund Freud, all of whom rejected the notion of soul, spirit, or even mental consciousness. Universities welcomed people like Alfred Kinsey, who made a mockery of human sexuality and dared to call what he did scientific research. These were to result in such idiotic programs as values clarification, consciousness raising, and diversity training in place of traditional studies in schools. In reality they were just disguised attempts to make room for feminism, homosexuality, humanism, and sundry other politically correct attitudes in the curriculum.

In the book *How Now Shall We Live,* Charles Colson said,

> The fact is that a utopian framework has taken away the conceptual tools we need to grapple with genuine evil. And when we cannot name or identify evil, we lose the capacity to deal with it. (4)

That is precisely where progressive education has brought

America. We can no longer identify evil. Evil to many Americans now means *not* embracing whatever lifestyle a person chooses, even when that lifestyle is clearly condemned in the Bible. Pro-life people are called evil by feminists and left-wing liberals. The Bible warns, "Woe to those who call evil good and good evil" (Isaiah 5:20). Many modern Americans reject the whole idea of evil because it means one has to accept the idea of a righteous standard for living which would be the opposite of evil. But as Colson noted, "In denying sin and evil, we actually unleash its worst powers." (5) Who can realistically look at society in America today and not recognize the truth of that statement? The worst powers of evil are at work in America to destroy faith, family, and freedom.

Any discussion of what has gone wrong with the direction of American education must look at where the progressive, pragmatic philosophies have influenced education practices in the nation. One must look especially at efforts to blur what exactly is being taught to make it more difficult for parents and others to examine the curriculums. When most teaching was done through textbooks and written scope and sequence guidelines were available, as in the past, at least parents had access to these if they so desired. However, most reform models of education advocate throwing out textbooks along with scope and sequence charts to allow more "freedom and flexibility in the classroom." This is always justified by claiming it is necessary in order to teach higher order thinking.

Kentucky's Education Reform Act of 1990 included the most massive changes to be undertaken by any state to date.

It was so complex that very few parents or even teachers were able to grasp the full impact. New responsibilities assigned to the schools would have thrilled the hearts of John Dewey and his followers. A look at how the reforms came about is interesting and leaves one with some unanswered questions.

In 1985 a lawsuit was brought against the governor, leaders of Congress, and others responsible for the distribution of funds for education in Kentucky. The suit, filed in Franklin Court by the "Council for Better Education," representing sixty-six school districts, claimed that inequitable and inadequate funds had been provided to those districts. In 1988 Judge Ray Corns ruled in favor of the school districts and ordered the governor and the General Assembly to devise a new system of funding to provide efficient and nondiscriminatory public education for the state.

It is surprising to note that rather than simply complying with Judge Corns' ruling, the defendants appealed the decision to the Kentucky Supreme Court. The court then issued an opinion in June, 1989, which held the entire school system of Kentucky unconstitutional, saying in part: "This decision applies to the entire sweep of the system—all its parts and parcels...the whole gamut of the common school system in Kentucky." It stated further, "We view this decision as an opportunity for the General Assembly to launch the Commonwealth into a new era of educational opportunity which will ensure a strong economic, cultural, and political future." (6)

In July, 1989 the leadership of the General Assembly appointed a task force to make recommendations on

PATRICIA MAYS

Curriculum, Governance, and Finance. A survey was subsequently done to find out what Kentucky wanted its children "to know and be able to do in the 21st century." The task force also hired consultant David Hornbeck to assist them in designing a completely new system of public education in Kentucky. Mr. Hornbeck, with ties to the Carnegie Foundation for the Advancement of Teaching, but not an educator himself, assured the state that their work would completely change the culture of schooling in Kentucky.

It appears somewhat curious that what started out to supposedly obtain equal funding for all students led to a complete change in curriculum, methodology, classroom organization, teacher certification, assessment, philosophy, goals and outcomes; in essence every area touching the schools in any way. It changed the role of elected boards of education and effectively eliminated the authority of an elected superintendent of public instruction in favor of an appointed commissioner. It mandated site-based councils composed of a principal along with teachers and parent representatives to govern each school. It ordered that family resource centers and youth services centers be established for all schools.

The work of the task force with the guiding hand of David Hornbeck culminated in an approximately one thousand page document known as House Bill 940, and was presented to the General Assembly in 1990. Governor Wallace Wilkinson, who had been willing to appeal a court decision which charged him to find a way to equally fund all districts, forced the General Assembly to vote on House

Bill 940 in the next legislative session along with all of the other legislation being considered at that time.

The governor refused to call a special session to consider such massive changes in education in the state. To have done so would have allowed legislators to take the legislation before the people before voting on it. As it was, the strongest voice legislators heard was that of representatives from the teachers' union, the Kentucky Education Association, an affiliate of the National Education Association. The Association was pushing for the legislation in order to gain that part of the reforms known as site-based management. This would effectively strip most power from elected school boards and give more power to teachers and their union.

Another part of the legislation would also remove most of the authority of the State Superintendent of Schools, elected by the public, and give it to an appointed Commissioner of Education. Obviously, the teachers' union could wield more influence over who would be appointed than they could over an elected official.

No one seems able to explain how it occurred that nearly everything contained in the reforms had been promoted by Governor Wilkinson's own Secretary of Education, Jack Foster, in the 1988 session, prior to the lawsuit which resulted in House Bill 940. The plan at that time was to establish twenty-one schools as pilot sites for the reforms. One has to take a second look at this to see the real problem. Supposedly the reforms presented in the bill were the culmination of a great many hours of work by a task force who based their entire findings on researching what Kentuckians wanted from the education system. But, their work mirrored exactly what had previously been promoted by Governor Wilkinson and quite clearly what had appeared in a plan presented to the Governor's Conference on Education in Hilton Head Island, South Carolina, prior to 1988.

Furthermore, it seems quite an amazing coincidence that this plan was voted into law in Kentucky, the only state in the nation where voters did not have the right to referendum, the right to recall, nor the right to petition. In other words, Kentucky was the only state where the constitution gave voters no way to get rid of unpopular legislation except by changing enough legislators who would then follow through with a commitment to vote the will of the people. There were certainly others aware of what was happening in Kentucky, and no doubt many governors were envious. Those involved in Kentucky's reforms had a sense of destiny and must have had a great deal of satisfaction at the thought that their names would go down in the history of education reform. United States Education Secretary Richard Riley called Kentucky's education reform "a lighthouse for the rest of the nation." (7) Consultant David Hornbeck told Kentucky's education task force that their work would change the culture of education in Kentucky. Perhaps a valid question to ask is whether the legislation was intended to change education or to change the culture of the state itself and of others who would follow its lead.

Human culture is the training, development, and refinement of mind, morals, and taste. It is defined as the sum total of the attainments and learned behavior patterns of any specific period, race or people. KERA, as the education reforms became known in Kentucky, more than any previous legislation, made the connection between education and a change in culture. It was designed to shape the future, but perhaps in ways that the citizens could not foresee. One state politician described the reforms as an "organic, living thing," which would "grow and evolve to meet circumstance in the real world of practice through a process of natural selection, just as living species do." (8)

Kentucky's curriculum framework was given the title "Transformations," meaning change. The framework consisted of two volumes containing just over five hundred pages each. Its stated purpose was "assuring that *each* child achieves the six learning goals identified in the Kentucky Education Reform Act." On page three of Volume I, it stated further that "Social, emotional, aesthetic, physical, and intellectual needs of students must be addressed in order to provide the optimum environment for learning." It is worth noting that this ordering placed the students' social needs first and academic needs last.

Kentucky's plan was to shape the total development of every child from the age of three years to the end of college. The Kentucky reforms went beyond the classroom. Also mandated was that every child have access to physical and mental health care through the schools. Family resource centers were to be established in every district to teach proper parenting and coping skills. It made available child care programs before and after school as well as during the summer. Year-round schools were pushed.

In May of 1992 Thomas Boysen, Kentucky's first appointed Education Commissioner under KERA, sent out a preliminary curriculum draft entitled, "Transforming

The Learning Environment Through Outcome-Based Education." It stated in part that, "This draft document presents the premises and principles to assist schools in implementation of OBE." Page four of Volume II of Kentucky's Curriculum Framework mentioned the "statewide commitment to an outcome-based approach to education," and page six of the same guide had a section titled, "Outcome Based Education: The Foundation of KERA."

The issue of outcome-based education is one which has been clouded by confusion. Probably very few people, including educators, could actually give a good working definition for the term. That may be because it has been used synonymously with other terms like "mastery learning," "performance-based education," "core curriculum," "valued outcomes," "quality performance standards," "re-learning," and "restructuring."

Simply stated, outcome-based education means that desired outcomes are specified and then tested periodically to see if adequate progress is being made. If the desired goal has not been met, re-teaching occurs, and then retesting. This process is repeated until mastery occurs. If it were really this simple in operation very few parents would be opposed to it.

The problem arises when the goals and outcomes to be attained are spelled out. Invariably these goals have been tied to feelings, beliefs, and attitudes, and separated from more traditional models where basic skills and knowledge are emphasized. Designers of outcome-based models begin with the question "What do we want students to know, do, and be like?" However, in the final answer to the question more emphasis is placed on what do we want students to *do* and *be like* than on what students should know. Then an attempt is made to initiate a system of total equality for all students.

While lip service is paid to individual ability and learning styles, the stated premise underlying the entire program is that "*all* students are expected to achieve the same goals and outcomes." Terms like "authentic assessment" and "acceptable demonstration of synthesized behaviors" begin to replace traditional achievement testing. This is defended by the reformers as necessary in order to move education away from what they believe to be the unsuccessful low-level teaching of the past, and to focus on the higher level cognitive skills of analysis, synthesis and evaluation.

"Teaching" suddenly becomes an outdated term linked to the passing of specific knowledge from one individual to others. The newer, more acceptable word facilitator, used frequently in re-training teachers under the Kentucky reforms, literally means one who makes things easier or more convenient. Favorable learner objectives include such verbs as decide, judge, choose, justify, persuade, defend, analyze, support, predict, and evaluate. Terms such as know, understand, and comprehend are devalued. Multiple-choice test items are allowed but given low-level priority. Emphasis is placed on open-ended or open-response type questions which have no right or wrong answers.

As in other states, Kentucky's reforms followed the National Education Standards. The wording of Kentucky's main goals and those of most other states have been almost verbatim those contained in the National Education Goals. Those eight goals progress from insuring that all children begin school ready to learn (programs for preschoolers and their parents,) through completion of high school. It continues with having all students achieve at high levels and prepared for citizenship, having American students at the top in mathematics and science worldwide, to adult literacy and lifelong learning. Also among the goals are those involving teacher professional development and assuring safe and disciplined, drug-free schools. What parent would not want these for his or her child?

On the surface they sound very worthy. However, as we judge politicians, or rather as we should judge them, not by what they say, but by the record of their accomplishments, we should also judge efforts to reform our education system by the proof of their success. Though the goals sound impressive, the proof is in the pudding, and as one looks at the specific outcomes that followed the broad goals and at the results, the proof is missing.

Kentucky's student performance record was to be a dismal one. Although the reform legislation threw out achievement testing in an effort to control perception of any damage, its replacement tests were so flawed, the state was unable to continue using them, and was eventually forced to reinstate achievement testing. Those results showed a totally different picture of performance than the state tests had suggested, and what it revealed was not good. When compared to the rest of the nation, Kentucky students made no significant gains in eight years despite higher spending per student, lower student-teacher ratio, and higher teacher salaries. Since by the reform proponent's own admission, Kentucky students had been near the bottom in achievement before the reforms, this was not music to anyone's ears.

Kentucky's reform plan included six major learner goals and outcomes, which all Kentucky students were expected to achieve. The following is a list of those goals in the order in which they occur in Kentucky's framework:

1. Students are able to use basic communication and mathematics skills for purposes and situations they will encounter throughout their lives.

2. Students shall develop their abilities to apply core concepts and principles from mathematics, the sciences, the arts, the humanities, social studies, practical living studies, and vocational studies, to what they will encounter throughout their lives.

3. Students shall develop their abilities to become self-sufficient individuals.

4. Students shall develop their abilities to become responsible members of a family, work group, or community, including demonstrating effectiveness in community service.

5. Students shall develop their abilities to think and solve problems in school situations and in a variety of situations they will encounter in life.

6. Students shall develop their abilities to connect and integrate experiences and new knowledge from all subject matter fields with what they have previously

learned, and build on past learning experiences to acquire new information through various media sources.

The most controversial of the goals were numbers three and four. Goal three, when spelled out, called for students to become self-sufficient by "having healthy self-esteem, a healthy lifestyle, by being adaptable and flexible and by making decisions based on ethical values." Goal four insisted that all students become "responsible" members of a family, work-group or community. Among the outcomes of goal four were those that stated that students must "demonstrate understanding of, appreciation for, and sensitivity to a multi-cultural and world view, and must demonstrate an open mind to alternative perspectives."

It is imperative that anyone examining the plan realize that under it students are required to *demonstrate* the outcomes in order to graduate from high school. Critics of the goals understandably questioned how proficiency in some areas could be objectively measured. Camille Wagner, of Parents and Professionals Involved in Education asked, "How much self-esteem is enough self-esteem?" and, "How adaptable and flexible are children going to be required by the state to be, and toward what beliefs?" (9) She wanted further clarification of "Where productive team member skills leave off and undue encouragement to submit to peer pressure begin?" (10) Wagner also stated concerns because parents, teachers, and elected school boards had no say in setting the standards for the non-academic outcomes.

Another important question brought up was how students who failed to demonstrate the outcomes would be remedied. So much attention to these questions was drawn by the efforts of parent and professional groups that the commissioner of education called for either dropping those goals altogether or not including them in the assessments. Perhaps there were hopes that once the other portions of the reforms were well established, these could be reinstated in the future with less notice.

While the first two goals for Kentucky appeared to be academic in nature and together encompassed seventy-two percent of the learner outcomes, one must not overlook the fact that the goals did not address the acquisition of knowledge or skills at all. Fifty-one percent of the academic outcomes fell under *application* of core concepts and principles and another twenty-one percent under the *ability to use* basic skills. Application of and use of are not the same as acquisition of skills, and traditionally have been expected to follow acquisition.

A table under the heading of "Curriculum" included in a Kentucky Education Reform Briefing Notebook described "How Learning Has Changed." It stated that learning has changed "from acquiring knowledge to using knowledge." It has changed "from one right answer to most appropriate answer," and "from scope and sequence to revisit skills and concepts at a higher, more complex level." It also stated that learning has changed "from learning in separate disciplines to learning across disciplines" and "from different standards for different students to high standards for all students." (11)

At the heart of any objective look at the goals of the Kentucky Education Reform Act is the question of whether or not a child must first acquire knowledge and skill before applying them. The word skill indicates the demonstration of one's ability or proficiency *acquired* through training and repetitive practice. It is the belief that children don't need to bother with "lower levels" of learning, and that all children are capable of higher order thinking that has a strong connection to metaphysics and the philosophy of existentialism. It is connected to the idea that all children are born with certain knowledge already in place. Teachers often hear or read things like: "Education is just leading out what is already in the child's soul." This is nonsense, especially if you take seriously the implications of naturalism, which denies the existence of a supernatural soul.

The lack of emphasis on acquisition of knowledge becomes evident as one looks at the instructional approaches proposed by the education reforms. Among the first visible changes to the classroom with the Kentucky reforms were the un-graded primary and the institution of whole language as the method of teaching reading and language arts to beginning students. Whole language was expected to bypass the need for pre-reading skills. Basal readers and skills workbooks were discarded. In place of these, students would use "trade books," or all sorts of children's literature books. Just think of the possibilities for influencing little minds when teachers or those above them could select whatever children's books fit their own philosophies and fill the classrooms with these. One would have to be naive indeed to think that all children's books are innocent. A realistic recognition of the infiltration of less than ideal role models into the classrooms in recent decades should give parents reason for concern.

Kentucky legislators and educators were assured that whole language had been proven to be the superior method of teaching reading and writing. They were convinced that because of the "overwhelming evidence" in favor of whole language over traditional methods, it should be mandated for every public primary classroom in the state.

However, Linda C. Fielding wrote in an article published in the *Encyclopedia of Education Research* that, "The difference in what counts as 'proof' to different members of the language arts professional community remains an issue on which professionals are sharply divided." (12) The article says that Stahl & Miller (1989) conducted a meta-analysis of studies that compared kindergarten and first grade basal reader-oriented and whole language experience-oriented programs. They concluded that whole language was more effective at kindergarten but not at first grade. (13) Phonics instruction was not mentioned, but even a basal reader approach was more effective than whole language at the first grade level, where children are expected to begin to read.

The research discussed above was reported the year before the Kentucky state department, in implementing the Kentucky Education Reform Act, declared that whole language instruction be used in every primary classroom in the state.

At the same time there was a massive experiment going on with whole language instruction in California. After ten years, the reading scores for California public school students were so bad that the legislature there mandated that all schools must include phonics instruction in the teaching of reading. Chances are, however, that California did not see a great jump in reading performance unless they first instructed their teachers in how to teach phonics. Most teachers do not understand phonics because they have never been taught it themselves. What will pass for phonics instruction in most cases will be haphazard at best, while successful programs follow a necessary progression.

Also mandated in the Kentucky Education Reform Act was the institution of an un-graded primary. Children were not to be assigned to a grade level, but rather several ages would be grouped together. In the beginning this combined kindergarten through third grade children. Later groupings were more likely to include only two age levels.

At the primary level, the reforms did away with assigning children grades for their work. Report cards were changed to a subjective type of checklist. Since objective tests were no longer to be given, teachers' observations were expected to be sufficient.

Teachers were allowed to assign grades for work in fourth through eighth grades, but since much of the work was to be done in cooperative groups and assessed through writing portfolios, grades took on a different meaning.

The Kentucky education reforms did not stop with its transformation of the lower grades. It also mandated that the state totally restructure the high schools. The Task Force of High School Restructuring in its final report on June 30, 1993 offered five "Core Components for High School Graduation":

1. Individual Graduation Plans

2. Integrated Academic Portfolios

3. Student-initiated Culminating Project

4. School-sponsored and -approved Activities

5. Exit Reviews

These five components would be required for all students and would replace the traditional subject units for graduation.

The *Individual Graduation Plan* required that, prior to entering high school, each student should develop an individual plan that "documents an academic program of study for achieving the six KERA Learning Goals and demonstrating the seventy-five Learner Outcomes." One needs to keep in mind that when fully implemented there would be no subject requirements—no units required for English, math, science, etc. All that was necessary was to "demonstrate" that the state's goals and outcomes had been met. Exactly how that was to be done was not even hinted at in the report.

The *Integrated Academic Portfolio* was to be a single portfolio from all courses and experiences throughout high school and submitted by the student to the appropriate teacher or educator panel. Work contained in the portfolio must "demonstrate the six state Learning Goals and the seventy-five Learner Outcomes."

A *Student-Initiated Culminating Project and Presentation* would include a major written component, and the student would be required to "perform, exhibit, demonstrate, or present the project to his/her panel." The student was to design the project prior to the anticipated final year of high school during the review process of the Individual Graduation Plan. Assessment of the project and presentation was to be "based on criteria established by the school council/district."

Each student was required to actively participate in at least one *School Sponsored and Approved Activity*. Activities would be "designated as such by the school council and/or the district board of education" who would be given the "freedom to determine the range of opportunities available," and the "procedure for awarding credit for completion of this component."

The *Exit Review* consisted of verification by school officials that "the components required for high school graduation have been met, including documentation of student achievement of the state's six Learning Goals and demonstration of the seventy-five Learner Outcomes."

In answer to the question why are these changes needed, the task force on restructuring gave these reasons:

Too many have not succeeded under the old system. A high school graduate needs to be able to see the connections across the disciplines, work well independently and in teams, solve problems in real settings, apply knowledge, prepare and re-educate for the possibility of several different careers, lead a healthy lifestyle, manage a successful family and serve our community as a productive and active citizen. (14)

It is easy to see from these goals an all-encompassing nature and the school's aim to completely shape every child for the envisioned society. (The mandates given to states under President Bush's "No Child Left Behind" policy may have caused a few changes to be made, especially since students would be expected to pass certain nationally recognized tests in order to graduate.)

Under "Assumptions and Beliefs of the Task Force" were the following:

1. Young people are valuable resources.

2. All students can learn and achieve at high levels.

3. All students should be taught at the highest level.

4. All students should be considered to be preparing for *each* of the following: college, vocational/technical school, the workplace (including the home as workplace), the military, and community service. This means that any program a school provides should be available to all students, and successful completion should lead to *all* post-secondary options.

5. Teaming of students (cooperative learning) and the adults who serve them is one necessary prerequisite to restructuring.

6. Curricular approaches should involve students in activities that have meaning to them.

7. Schools must respect and celebrate diversity in race, class, and gender.

8. School rules should be continually reconsidered to prevent their being used inappropriately to limit student abilities. (15)

It is important to look closely at assumptions number three and four. If completely implemented it would mean that no advanced class could be offered in high school unless every student (regardless of ability) could successfully complete it. It is difficult to imagine a trigonometry or calculus class that could be successfully completed by a child with an IQ of seventy (or lower). How about an advanced literature class for students who not only couldn't read but could not comprehend? One has to keep in mind, however, that the emphasis is always on collaborative learning, and students are not held individually responsible. Also, if grades are given at all, they are re-defined. Actually, the framers of this philosophy saw no problem because advanced classes would not exist. There would be no subject divisions because all course work would be combined across disciplines. All activities would have to have a functional nature; theory would have no place in such a scheme. It must be kept in mind that under this philosophy what has meaning for one person may not hold interest for another, and teachers were expected to plan for that.

Under "Themes for Student Success" (16), the task force included the requirement of "success for all students." They further recommended that "the approach to curriculum, instruction, and assessment be performance-based across disciplines as opposed to primarily knowledge or skill-based." It required that students collaborate with each other to "help them become part of a community of learners." Textbooks were to be used as resources only along with resources outside the classroom.

"Assessment based upon performance, exhibition, and demonstration" were major parts of the program. (17) "Performance tests" were instituted at the fourth and eighth grade levels with the beginning of the Kentucky Education Reform Act's implementation. Perhaps a look at how those worked would help explain what the task force was referring to as "performance-based curriculum, instruction, and assessment."

Trained examiners were sent to all elementary and middle schools to administer the performance assessments. They set up a room, often in the school library, and had the classes brought in. The students were randomly grouped with three to five students to a group and sent to different areas representing the different disciplines. One group might be given a problem to solve involving the use of math, for instance: "Design and plan for a construction project, designing blueprints and scale drawings to explain the project and to sell it."

All students in the group were expected to participate, and the group was to write out how they went about completing the project. Students were given approximately thirty minutes to work as a group. At the signal from the facilitator, the students would stop their group work and begin their individual work. Each student would then answer the problem the group had been working on and explain how they came to their conclusions.

One important thing to notice is that the students

assigned to the math group may or may not be good math students. Some may be learning disabled or even mentally handicapped. There may or may not be a student in the group who is a leader and who understands written directions well. They may or may not have someone who can write well enough to explain their work. However, this group would be responsible for the math performance score for the entire grade at this school. That score would then be compared with the score the following year for a different group of randomly assigned students from the same grade to see if the school's score had improved.

One teacher at my school, who also wrote for the town newspaper, wrote about an incident when his eighth grade class was taking the performance test. His class was told to prepare for the science test, but when facilitators for the testing company arrived they had substituted an art test for the science test without any warning. The teacher later found out that all of the science tests had been replaced with an art test because the company had found some sort of problem with them. The students were expecting to take a science test and had been studying for it all year. (18) These were just a few of the many problems that eventually led to dropping the performance tests from the school's accountability score.

Another recommendation of the task force was that schools have the discretion to reduce the number of students that teachers were responsible for. They were expected to do this by reorganizing scheduling, using blocks of time, and dividing the school into houses, clusters or schools within schools. Most parents and educators would probably agree that a smaller group of students working with a group of teachers who know them well is a good idea. This was once achieved in the smaller community schools. As small community schools were swallowed up in consolidation, high school teachers were required to teach as many as one hundred fifty students a day.

Under the reform proposals for high school restructuring, the requirements for teaching would be redefined. Instead of major/minor areas of concentration, teachers would be prepared to work in teams, across subject areas, and in a "performance-oriented" (or activities) environment. Teachers would become "catalysts, guides, facilitators, questioners, and coaches, not dispensers of facts and rules." (19) This appeared a bit contradictory or at least removed from findings that part of the problem with our middle and high school performance on national and international tests was that teachers were not well-trained in the discipline they were teaching. Many were teaching in areas outside their college majors and did not have a deep understanding of the material.

In the spring of 1999, the State Department of Education in Kentucky announced that new standards would be set for classroom specialists. It had been brought out that several classroom specialists in the state were not qualified in the academic area they were supposed to be leading. Education specialists were supposed to be sent out to any school that had not demonstrated sufficient progress according to their state test scores. One such specialist sent to aid schools in language arts instruction was a health and physical education teacher with "no teaching certification and no classroom experience." (20) At least two others were employed as experts for social studies teachers but without any social studies credentials themselves. It is interesting to note that these "specialists" were earning about $14,000 more per year than they would have made as a classroom teacher.

Teachers at all levels were to be trained differently in Kentucky. The law established an "Education Professional Standards Board" to oversee everything involving the preparation and licensing of teachers in order to link these to state changes in the classroom. Universities in Kentucky were encouraged to eliminate what was referred to as an undergraduate major in teacher education. All teacher candidates would be required to receive a baccalaureate in a particular academic discipline, although there was no clear delineation of how teachers would be placed on the basis of that particular area of study. In fact, the language of the reforms appeared to discourage the teaching by division of disciplines.

Colleges and universities would be "free to develop programs that will help students meet standards without regard to specific courses or credit hours." (21) Prospective teachers would be judged by academic portfolios, scheduled performance events, and standardized tests. They were encouraged to take a series of courses consisting of "information and experiences related to understanding children and their families, the structure and functions of schools, and the implications of the Kentucky Education Reform Act for teachers and students." (22) The standards board also recommended that "alternative preparation programs be made available for persons experienced in other fields to pursue teaching careers." (23)

The Reform Act turned education upside down in the state of Kentucky. Parents and teachers alike were blind sided with an overwhelming and confusing re-defining of schooling. Teachers had to be re-educated by spending countless hours learning how to re-invent the wheel and then how to assess it even before it was finished. One state official was reported to have said, "We are flying the airplane as it is being made." Not surprisingly, many parents were hesitant to trust their children's safety to such a machine.

If Kentucky's experiment were contained to one state, it would not be worth the attention given here. However, reforms in Kentucky were based on the national model desired by education leaders and politicians. It would not only change the culture of education in Kentucky, it would affect what would be taught in the universities to future educators. Also, other states would be attempting the same changes in their own education framework.

As will be demonstrated in a subsequent chapter, Kentucky's grand experiment in changing the culture of education resulted in many casualties. Academic scores dropped dramatically when they were finally assessed through objective tests. However, the role of schools had been forever changed to accommodate the progressives' vision for shaping the future of American education.

"The crucible for silver and the furnace for gold, but the Lord tests the heart."

(Proverbs 17:3)

TRUTH IN TESTING

How do we know what children know?

One of the major problems with outcome-based programs in reform efforts is that parents know very little about what their children are being taught. It is impossible for the local school board or the state to monitor the content of the curriculum. Furthermore, many testing experts agree that test objectives for outcome-based programs are often vague and difficult to assess reliably. For example, learner outcome 2.27 in Kentucky's curriculum framework stated, "Students complete tasks, make presentations, and create models that demonstrate awareness of the diversity of forms, structures, and concepts across languages and how they may interrelate." Learner outcome 6.3 said, "Students expand their understanding of existing knowledge (e.g. topic, problem situation, product) by making connections with new and unfamiliar knowledge, skills, and experiences." Some educators may know exactly what to do from these objectives, but most outsiders will be totally befuddled by them.

Another major problem with the idea of such programs evolving over time is that while they are evolving, there will be many casualties. Anything goes, as long as the schools do well on the state tests. One father related to me that the only thing he knew for sure his daughters had learned was that the white men stole from and corrupted the Indian's way of life. They had been working with this theme for several years. Native America has been a favorite theme for most elementary classrooms because it can be taught so colorfully. Children can learn how to make Indian jewelry, pottery, and rugs. They can learn Indian songs and dances and write poetry about the animals, trees, and rocks. Children can use rocks, shells, and feathers for mathematics as well as art activities. It is even possible to bring in some Native American religion.

It is not difficult to see that it would be possible to bring in anything of interest to the teacher if it can be developed into a theme and applied to reading and writing activities. A July, 1997 article from the Los Angeles Associated Press reported on some teachers there who were using Scientology in their classrooms, and were hoping to start a charter school with tax funds using the methods. As a charter school they would be allowed to operate outside many state and district rules that constrain curriculums and budgets. The teachers referred to the methods they were using as "Applied Scholastics" and made no mention of their origin when they made their proposal for charter school status.

A thorough investigation of the outcome-based models of education reveals the unmistakable fact that whoever controls the test controls the curriculum. Teachers and administrators have expressed concern that legislation under "No Child Left Behind" pushes the schools to teach to the test.

Teaching to the test was what the Kentucky Education Reform Act was all about. The goal of teaching in Kentucky schools was to achieve demonstration of the seventy-five learner outcomes. Since the outcomes dealt with doing, behaving, and feeling rather than with acquisition of knowledge and skills, they could not be tested through traditional objective tests. At the primary level, assessment was to be accomplished by the use of "anecdotal records," "conferencing," "portfolios," and other teacher created "authentic assessment" strategies.

The state test, known as the Kentucky Instructional Results Information System or KIRIS, was given only to grades four, eight, and twelve (later changed to grade eleven) for accountability purposes, meaning that performance at these grade levels determined the school's score, and whether the school should receive rewards or sanctions. Rewards were given every two years to teachers and administrators of schools that showed significant improvement, and schools with declining scores could be sanctioned, put on probation, have teachers and principals moved or replaced, and be under the supervision of a team of "specialists" from the state department. The test contained three parts:

1. Performance tasks (removed from accountability score after five years because of criticisms over reliability.)

2. Portfolios

3. Multiple choice and open-ended response questions

(The state department removed Multiple choice questions in 1994.)

Scoring for the tests consisted of a four point rating system. The lowest rating of "novice" was followed by "apprentice" and "proficient." "Distinguished" was the very highest performance level. It was stressed to teachers and parents that under this system, no child would fail. The lowest level of achievement merely showed him or her to be a beginner, not a failure.

Schools were rated according to what percentage of students fell into each rank on a scale of zero to one hundred forty. The goal was to get each school to achieve a rank of one hundred with an average number of students at the proficient level and an equal number on either side at apprentice and distinguished. Each year schools set their own goals for improvement, and monetary rewards were given to schools that made sufficient improvement in their scores. Schools which failed to make sufficient progress were subject to sanctions, and the state could send a "distinguished educator" to guide the school toward improvement. Principals and teachers could be removed if the state so desired.

The state immediately embarked on a frenzied push to sell the test and the reforms to the teachers and administrators. Literature and carefully worded surveys hemorrhaged out of Frankfort. Most of them appealed to the educators' pride in being at the forefront of real education progress in the nation. There was plenty of rhetoric about the research behind the proven superiority of the methods. The spin job coming out of the state capital would have made the Clinton White House envious.

When asked whether the state's tests correlated highly with well-known standardized tests, the Kentucky Department of Education responded that "the correlation between the state's assessments and well-known traditional tests fall between fifty percent and seventy-five percent." Higher correlations they said, "could mean that the state test is not going far enough beyond traditional tests to measure what students can do with their knowledge." (1) They reported correlations with the NAEP and CTBS tests varying from sixty-three percent to eighty-six percent. They admitted, however, that the correlations with the American College Test ranged from thirty percent in science to fifty-four percent in mathematics. (2)

The state discouraged districts from giving standardized tests, and those who did so must bear the expense themselves. Some districts did give them and with considerable differences in correlation than those reported by the education department. In Christian County, Lacy Elementary School scored so low on the state test in 1996 that it was labeled a "school in decline," and was in danger of having sanctions imposed. Then, in the spring of 1997 the CTBS was given to students in the third, sixth, and ninth grades. Lacy students scored above the fiftieth percentile nationwide and better than all but one other elementary school in the district, while the school that had scored the highest on Kentucky's state test received only a national percentile score of thirty-nine and three tenths, indicating that nearly six of every ten schools nationwide did better.

In 1995 the Lexington Herald-Leader reported that the performance of the state's fourth graders who took the national reading test in 1994 scored lower than the fourth graders who took it in 1992, though the drop, they said, was not significant. What it did show was that the state's fourth graders had not made the improvements in reading that the state had claimed. In contrast to the national test, "Results released in September from Kentucky's own tests showed that the state's fourth graders improved their reading scores by eighty-nine percent over that same time." (3)

In October of 1998, the state released scores from the California Test of Basic Skills, required of the three grades tested for accountability. The results showed Kentucky third graders at forty-nine and eight tenths on the total battery. It was fifty and two-tenths for sixth graders, and forty-eight and eight tenths for ninth grade, below the national average on two of the three and just barely average on the other. This is the great progress made after ten years of reforms and millions of extra tax dollars to improve education in Kentucky. An important thought to remember at this point is that it was a hard-fought battle to get a nationally normed test given again to students across the state, so that comparisons could be made.

What have the reforms in Kentucky accomplished? The answer depends on whom you ask. The Kentucky School Boards Association publicly complained that, "the standards on which the reforms are based are not understandable and do not focus enough on academics." (4) The first of two studies of the Kentucky testing system, done by testing experts at Western Michigan University, listed the following as problems:

1. Teaching to the test may narrow curriculum.

2. Students with content knowledge but inadequate writing skills may have little chance to do well.

3. Tests do not provide parents with reliable results showing how individual students performed.

4. The test's reliability is insufficient to decide rewards and sanctions. (5)

The second study said, "Kentucky's assessment and accountability system is seriously flawed and needs to be substantially revised." (6) They declared the performance-based tests to be unreliable, particularly pertaining to bias in scoring of portfolios. One of the test reviewers said the group was "guardedly optimistic that the portfolios may be effective for instruction." Regarding the use of portfolios for testing he added, "But we ended up unanimously negative in terms of the appropriateness of portfolio scores for use in the current accountability system." (7) The reviewer was referring to problems with upward bias in the scoring of portfolios, and the inconsistency of scoring from school to school. He went on to say that, "They're giving their kids scores higher than other evidence suggests the kids deserve." (8) Nevertheless, the state continued to use the scores to dole out $26 million in rewards every two years to schools that made the greatest gains. Most schools that received the rewards split up the bonuses among their faculty, administrators, and certified personnel.

Questions had been raised when Jefferson County released results from the California Test of Basic Skills given to students there that showed declining scores in math and reading over the past three years, while the state's own test showed students improving dramatically in the same subject areas. A poll of teachers in 1995 made public in 1996 linked test gains to coaching, not improved learning. "Teachers reported questionable test-administration practices... including teachers rephrasing questions, answering questions about content, recommending revisions and giving hints on correct answers during test time." (9)

In July of 1997 the *Lexington Herald-Leader* reported that "the state had failed to investigate dozens of reported cases of cheating on the tests." (10) The following November a Jessamine County elementary school that had earned ninety-three thousand dollars for high test scores in recent years was cited for cheating. Teachers had taken notes on the tests from a curriculum resource teacher. "State officials analyzed the test scores from 1991 to 1997 and found an 'extremely high correlation' between the notes and individual questions." (11) It was not immediately decided whether the school would have to return the reward money to the state. Other schools were cited for various irregularities including tip sheets based on actual test questions and lack of security for test materials. It was reported that some students had even been allowed to work on the test at home. A principal from Bell County who had won a twenty-five thousand dollar Milken Educator Award for Excellence in 1993 was moved to the county's alternative school after his school's test scores were thrown out because of test irregularities. It wasn't clear whether or not he was allowed to keep the money.

In 1997, the first year that a standardized test was given statewide since the reforms, and comparisons to the state's own test showed considerable differences, the state department announced that a "programming glitch" had caused the state's test contractor for Kentucky's state test to report wrong scores for many schools in the state. Because of these errors, scores for most schools had to be recalculated making thirty-two additional schools and five entire districts eligible for rewards. The same week, the state department announced that documentation on how the testing company had arrived at scores for eighth-grade vocational studies/practical living tests was missing. In 1998 state tests were criticized for typographical errors and missing grids on answer sheets. After so many errors were made public, the state's Parent Teacher Association announced that it was asking the state to allow an independent agency to take over testing, saying that the state department had lost credibility.

The state legislature did respond to the public outcry and finally ordered the Department of Education to come up with a new test that would be able to demonstrate reliability and validity. One of the most challenging responsibilities of the advisory council was to determine how schools would be held accountable for results. According to an Associated Press writer, among the "embarrassing anomalies" the state wanted to put behind it with the new testing system were the following:

1. Schools with consistently high scores that were classified "in decline" or "in crisis" because they slipped slightly one year or made only minute gains for three in a row.

2. Schools with low scores that qualified for cash rewards by ringing up big gains from a rock-bottom baseline.

3. "Free rider" teachers who avoided the grades used for accountability, but shared their schools' reward money. (12)

Talking with teachers about the success of Kentucky's reforms got varied results. Some teachers were very enthusiastic about the changes, while others confidentially expressed deep concerns over the falling levels of basic skill acquisition they saw in their students. Teachers could only express their concerns in strictest confidence because the state legislature had warned that teachers who publicly criticized the reforms could be subject to dismissal.

One fourth grade teacher estimated that her incoming students (after the first couple of years under the reforms) were about a year behind on their math skills. Another fourth grade teacher who gave her own tests to students at the beginning of the year found that many could not even do basic addition or subtraction without a calculator.

In the spring of 1994, an informal survey of a group of primary teachers in my county was conducted. Of the seventeen teachers who returned the survey, several were enthusiastic about the reforms, but not a single teacher felt that the testing system could be trusted to measure accurately the achievement of their students.

When asked if their students were learning to read more effectively than previous classes (before reforms), fifty-three percent said no, while twenty-nine percent were unsure. Forty-one percent said their students did not understand mathematical concepts as well as previous classes and twenty-four percent were not sure. While fifty-three percent of the respondents felt their students' computational skills were lower than previous classes, the majority (fifty-eight percent) did think their students were more able to express their ideas in writing. Portfolios were a major part of the assessments toward accountability for teachers and schools, so naturally more effort had to be placed on writing. However, that still left forty-two percent of the surveyed teachers not totally convinced that students were even doing better in the area most stressed by the reforms.

One parent told me that one of their two daughters is gifted intellectually while the other is an average student. On the Kentucky Test given to primary students, their children received exactly the same assessment on their performance. Since the gifted child is also highly motivated to achieve, this is hard to explain. Another parent whose child was struggling with reading, and whose standardized test scores later showed him to be one and one-half years behind grade level, obtained a high score in reading on the Kentucky test. Another parent was told by her daughter's teacher that the child would be making A's in reading if grades were given, but the parent found out when her daughter was tested independently that this fourth grade child was actually only able to read at a first grade level. Later the child was labeled as having dyslexia.

Kentucky's Department of Education worked ceaselessly to control the damage of bad publicity. They did all sorts of acrobatics with statistics to make it look as if Kentucky's schools had improved under the Kentucky Education Reform Act. However, the facts just didn't support such a conclusion. Kent Ostrander, Executive Director for The Family Foundation in Kentucky, pointed out the discrepancy in the Education Department's slant on the results of the 1998 National Assessment of Education Progress (NAEP). It was reported that the state showed significant gains over the 1994 test. However, the Department failed to release the information that showed the state had excluded 250 percent more students with disabilities from taking the 1998 test. Ostrander quoted NAEP's own officials as saying that when means were adjusted for the increase in student exclusions, Kentucky's gain was not statistically significant. (13)

In the summer of 1999, the Pritchard Committee for Academic Excellence, a group that had been a frequent cheerleader for Kentucky's education reforms in the beginning, blasted the state for its "atrocious middle school scores." (14) The group also reportedly estimated that "half of the state's fourth-graders are inadequate readers," and that "the state is not doing enough to help students get basic reading skills before they leave the fourth grade." (15) Remember, this was after nine years of dramatic reforms that were going to sail Kentucky to the top of the nation. The results hardly sound like progress.

The June 1994 Hudson Briefing Paper on "Shaping the Future" documented how Kentucky's encounter with outcome-based education paralleled what had been happening all over the country. It stated that twenty-five states had developed or implemented outcome-based education and that eleven others had made outcomes a part of the state accreditation or assessment process. The article showed how transformational Outcome-Based Education (a name applied by William G. Spady, the man most often associated with its model) "actually makes accountability impossible." (16) It goes on to say that "The fundamental problem with the outcomes being proposed by Spady and others is in their conception of the purpose and role of education...that it is possible and justifiable for educators to create a new social order." (17) As has already been stated, goals and outcomes defined by outcome-based models are always tied to feelings, beliefs, and attitudes. Emphasis is placed on what students should do and be like, rather than on what they should know.

An organization of parents and professionals involved in education was able to glean a look at some of the types of questions used on the state tests for accountability. They reported reading stories with depressing themes and stories that discouraged having high hopes as with "The Frogs at the Rainbow's End" where some frogs looking for the rainbow's end fall prey to a snake that eats them up. The story's moral was given as "The highest hopes may lead to the greatest disappointments." Open-ended response questions in some cases asked questions that would reveal children's attitudes toward such things as role reversal as in the story "Your Dad's A Wimp." These stories were intended for fourth graders. Some eighth graders reported being asked open-ended response questions about such things as how much peer pressure it would take to cause them to change the way they usually act.

One of the problems test reviewers found with the Kentucky test was the de-emphasis of subject matter knowledge, especially for science and social studies. The report stated that "it was almost as though the student did not have to attend science or social studies classes to be able to answer the questions." (18)

Donna Shedd, vice-president of Eagle Forum of Kentucky, and former Republican nominee for State Superintendent of Public Instruction, published an article entitled "Anyone Paying Attention to keragate?!" (19) In it she listed some of the evidence that the reforms in Kentucky were not working as the promoters would have the tax payers believe. Among those were the following:

1. The American College Test's findings that the KERA test was not individually reliable

2. The Western Michigan University study that showed a deficiency in teaching basic skills, narrowing of curriculum, lack of validity and reliability.

3. NAEP test's disagreement with the KERA test on improvement in reading scores at the fourth grade. (KERA test showed eighty-nine percent improvement, NAEP test showed none.)

4. Panel of testing experts from around the country found the results of KERA testing had been overstated, exaggerated, misleading, and misinforming.

Despite all this evidence and criticism, the state extended the contract with the testing company for another year, and twenty-six million dollars in rewards would be given out by using the same criteria.

When the General Assembly finally decided that in view of the widespread negative publicity about the state test, a new test would have to be forthcoming, the state Department of Education seemingly didn't know where to begin or what to do. Three times within twelve months the department found itself without anyone to head up the redesign process.

Public school enrollment in Kentucky experienced some sharp drops after the reforms took place. Parents unhappy with the results began seeking an alternative. It was estimated that there was a thirty percent increase in the number of Kentucky students leaving the public schools.

The reforms in Kentucky have been described in detail in the hopes that readers can see where public education has been headed in this country. The rest of the nation was watching Kentucky with plans underway already in most states to copy at least parts of it in their own reforms. Over time, states using outcome-based models are usually forced to retreat to more traditional methods of educating, at least for a while, but that won't be the end of it. The attempts always return in some form, and it seems that each time they do, they get a little further than the last time. The philosophies behind these are now firmly entrenched in the fabric of public schools through those at the top of the education hierarchy and the politicians who are in league with them. It is not difficult to see that whoever controls the tests has control of the curriculum, and the curriculum under outcome-based models will always be spread through with politically correct propaganda. It will also be largely beyond the knowledge and control of parents.

Parents need to be ever vigilant concerning what their children are learning in school. This is true of private and parochial schools as well as public schools. Not every "Christian" school can be trusted to give children the very best education and to be consistent in applying Christian principles to the education process. This is especially true at the university level.

Worldviews based on falsity and error are a moral cancer in our nation whose tentacles are firmly wrapped into the fiber of our public education system. We can try to ignore them, but they will continue their destruction from within until our society collapses. Francis A. Schaeffer said in his book *A Christian Manifesto* that humanism and Christianity "are two total concepts of reality standing in antithesis to each other." (20) He continued,

> What we must understand is that the two worldviews really do bring forth with inevitable certainty not only personal differences, but also total differences in regard to society, government, and law. There is no way to mix these two total worldviews. They are separate entities that cannot be synthesized. (21)

Schaeffer believed that it was because of the failure of Christians to recognize that difference that we have arrived at the confused, decaying, and dying condition of the Western culture. He said that Christians must bear some of the responsibility for the fact that "the humanist world view...today controls the consensus in society, much of the media, much of what is taught in our schools, and much of the arbitrary law being produced by the various departments of government." (22) Schaeffer recognized that true Christians must begin to take notice of and deal with the fact that those currently in control of public education and other aspects of our government

> who hold the material-energy, chance concept of reality...not only do not know the truth of the final reality, God, they do not know who Man is. Their concept of Man is what Man is not. Since their concept of Man is mistaken, their concept of society and of law is mistaken, and they have no sufficient base for either society or law. (23)

We have arrived at a time when our society, including many of those who call themselves Christian, have come to believe that we can and ought to have a totally secular society, that religion is irrelevant and must only be allowed to exist outside of the public arena. Francis Schaeffer quoting a section from Will and Ariel Durant's book, *The Lessons of History*, said, "If Rationalism wishes to govern the world without regard to the religious needs of the soul, the experience of the French Revolution is there to teach us the consequences of such a blunder." (24) The Durants were professed humanists, but Schaeffer quoted their admission that, "There is no significant example in history, before our time, of a society successfully maintaining moral life without the aid of religion." (25)

If humanists themselves recognize the importance of religion in society, what means do they propose to use in restoring that which will help to maintain moral life? They certainly will not base that religious control upon true Christianity. And, what means will they use to propagate their new religion? Who could deny that public education would be the perfect vehicle?

"Discipline your son, for in that there is hope; do not be a willing party to his death."

(Proverbs 19:18)

TRUTH ABOUT DISCIPLINE

Why is spanking now taboo in America?

In years gone by, children were taught to respect authority. Young people were told by parents that if they got into trouble at school, they would be in worse trouble when they came home. The atmosphere today is nothing remotely similar. Schools are forced to spend a great deal of effort and time dealing with discipline problems. Students have become increasingly more unruly and disruptive. They have become more violent toward each other and teachers and administrators. To make things even worse, many parents defend their rebellious children and work against the school. Most teachers and school administrators are familiar with the saying, "Everyone wants discipline in the schools unless it is their own child who is being disciplined." This is too often the case, and it complicates further an already overwhelming job for school authorities.

Discipline is one of the most necessary elements in life. Discipline and love go hand in hand. The Bible says that the Lord disciplines all those he loves just as a father disciplines a child if he truly loves him (Revelation 3:19 and Deuteronomy 8:5). Hebrews 12:11 explains that discipline is not something we enjoy, but it seems painful to us. Though many well-meaning people have a hard time equating discipline and punishment, there has to be a connection at times. This is difficult to get away from, especially when we look at the verses in Proverbs. A lot of people try to make "the rod" it speaks of a synonym for verbal correction. Sometimes it may be. However, in Proverbs we are told, "if you punish the child with the rod, he will not die," and you will "save his soul from death" (Proverbs 23:13–14).

Good discipline has to begin early in life, just as soon as a child can understand the meaning of the word no. For the first few years of life, spanking—when used in the right way and at the right times—can be an excellent motivator. Compassionate discipline must always be done for the child's benefit, not to suit the whims of a frustrated parent. Physical punishment should never be applied in a state of anger. There is never an excuse for abusing a child in the name of discipline. Neither should spanking be the first course of action. Parents should always make sure a child understands what the rules are and that the parent is setting boundaries for him out of love, to keep him away from danger. In Proverbs 22:15, Solomon tells us that, "folly is bound up in the heart of a child, but the rod of discipline will drive it far from him." Folly or foolishness means the failure to acknowledge God and his authority, and as such, it leads to ultimate death and destruction. What loving parent would not want to spare the child they love from that? However, parents have been robbed of necessary tools for disciplining their children. They have been lied to by the so-called experts, and led to believe that children are basically good, and to be a good parent all you have to do is make sure your child feels loved and accepted.

Permissiveness has saturated our culture for more than a generation, and violence, cynicism, and disrespect in our society are the direct result. Many leaders are now recognizing that the trend needs to be reversed, but they still don't understand the truth about how to get the job done. They now acknowledge the need to set and enforce boundaries, but are unwilling to even consider that they made a big mistake in removing the threat of physical punishment. It's interesting to study the trials of Job in the Old Testament. Satan's first assault against Job was to remove his blessings. Job was such a man of integrity that he wouldn't sin by charging God foolishly in this. Then Satan said to God that Job was only remaining righteous because he hadn't been touched physically. Job's grief over the resulting physical trials was "very great" (Job 2:13). The next thirty-four chapters are a record of his suffering. Admittedly, there is much more to the interpretation of the book of Job, and it may be a stretch to apply this to the notion of chastening a child. The Bible clearly shows Job as a righteous man. However, the point is that God did not visit and speak to Job until he was fully broken. It was at that time that Job was the most teachable. It is important for parents to recognize that sometimes they have to first break a child's rebellious will and get her attention before she will listen to correction.

The so-called experts of the past generation bear a lot of the blame for what has happened to our families. They have made many parents feel guilty about disciplining their child and led them to wait too long before taking action. By the time they do, they are much more likely to abuse their child. Surely, the verbal abuse, anger, and neglect that occur too often are far more damaging to a child than a well-placed spanking. After correction of any kind, it is important for a child to be reassured of a parent's love and respect.

What works in the home also works in the school. It must be kept in mind that schools are acting in place of the parent. They are there to act as the parent in the education of the child. The same lack of discipline in the home is evidenced in the schools. Teachers and principles spend a great deal of time trying to just keep things under control enough so that learning can occur. Disruptions in the classroom are daily events. In some schools the unruliness is so bad that teachers are afraid of their own students.

There have always been rebellious children, but the problem of disruptive, unruly, and defiant children is much worse than in earlier generations. The founders of America warned that failure to teach children religious truth would result in moral breakdown. Discipline problems in schools accelerated rapidly after prayer and the Ten Commandments were forbidden. Children have been led to believe that there is no religious basis for right and wrong. They have been taught that they must decide their own standards for behavior. They have witnessed a culture that says, "if it feels good, do it." They have been subjected to self-esteem programs that cause them to focus too much attention on self while denying them the opportunity to earn legitimate self-respect. They have been led to believe that they should never be punished for anything they do.

As has already been stated, parents have been misled by the so-called experts in child rearing. Unfortunately so have educators. They have been told that children will eventually respond to reasoning and plenty of "love." By the time parents and teachers realize that no amount of reasoning with some children will lead to compliance, they have become so frustrated that sooner or later anger takes over, and then they are more likely to abuse a child. Parents and teachers have been told that punishment is wrong, and that physical punishment teaches children that it's okay to hit others. What foolishness! Most children recognize a deserved spanking. Furthermore, the Bible teaches that when you, "Flog a mocker...the simple will learn prudence..." (Proverbs 19:25).

The attitude that pervades our society says there is no place in an educated, progressive society for punishment. This is why we see lax sentences handed down to notorious criminals, and particularly when the crime is sexual in nature. Bill O'Reilly on the Fox News Channel has done several stories in recent months on liberal judges handing down ridiculously short or non-existent sentences for child predators. One judge made the pathetic statement that the child abuser should not be punished because he had "a sickness." It is no coincidence that laxity in our judicial sentencing has occurred at the same time as efforts to ban spanking of children. This mindset is not meant just for the schools. There has been for several years a push to ban the use of spanking by parents.

In most states, corporal punishment in schools has been totally eliminated. Current thinking is that punishment of any kind is a poor motivator. Teachers and parents have been made to feel guilty if they cannot keep children under control with positive re-enforcers. Certainly, there is a place in the classroom as well as the home for positive reinforcement of good behavior.

By positive reinforcement, educators mean actions or rewards that are appealing enough to a child for him or her to repeat a desired behavior until it becomes established. Parents and teachers using this method to increase good behavior face the challenge of finding a re-enforcer stronger than competing ones. For instance, a student may find the approval of his peers a much stronger incentive than the reward being offered for more positive behavior. In this case it may take the removal of peer reinforcement before positive measures can succeed.

If reinforcement is to work it has to be something the child values. Those in authority must first find out what "turns on" this particular child. What appeals to one child may not appeal to another. Then the reward must correspond in value with the behavior expected. For instance, telling a child "If you do everything I say all week, I'll buy you a candy bar at the end of the week," obviously wouldn't work. The child has to believe the task is possible, and the reward has to be something worth the effort required. Then, the connection must be made between the reward and the behavior. Waiting too long after the behavior has occurred before giving the reward weakens the response connection. It also runs the risk of reinforcing a later improper behavior. For instance, if the child was promised a popsicle for picking up her toys, and Mom has waited until Susie, having asked for her popsicle repeatedly, finally throws a tantrum, Mom may reinforce the tantrum by giving Susie the treat then.

Gradual removal of re-enforcers is important in this kind of behavior management system. Once the desired behavior is occurring regularly one should try reinforcing every two times the behavior occurs, then maybe every three or four times. In between, the use of natural reinforcements such as praise, a smile, pat or other encouragement should be given. The child should be associating praise, a smile, etc., with the pleasantness of a more tangible reward. In fact these social re-enforcers should be given whenever appropriate behavior occurs. Though it may not be possible to do this in every instance, it should be happening often.

With older children token systems may work better than treats. With this method, the child receives the token (a star, or hole punched on a card or chart, or a chip, piece of play money, etc.), which can be exchanged for something tangible at a later time. A school could even plan a carnival or festival of some sort where the children can use their earned points as tickets for their favorite games or booths. Some schools give children a free afternoon with a movie and treats if they have earned it with their good behavior. Other schools take a merit day once every grading period. Those who have earned it take the school day off and go on an enjoyable trip such as bowling, skating, or swimming. Those with poor behavior must stay at school and do extra work of some kind. The key is to make sure that every child knows that the privilege has truly been earned. If the other children know that Johnny didn't earn it, but is getting to take part anyway because his parent raised a stink, it undermines the whole program. In any school there will be parents who don't want to allow their child to suffer consequences of bad behavior or to be deprived of anything no matter what their behavior has been. School officials must present a united front and follow through with what they have said they would do. For this reason, the school should take proper effort to inform parents and students well in advance. Parents and students could even be asked to sign a contract at the outset of the program stating that they have been made aware of the expectations and rules of the game.

In such programs, parents should be notified on a daily or weekly basis of how the child is doing. A behavior sheet in a folder or a notebook type agenda make it easier for the teacher to make notations each day. Parents can be required to sign these on a daily basis. If this behavior journal is joined with the record of homework assignments, and the parent must sign or initial, it is even more beneficial. Care must be taken here to be sure that the child is not held accountable for the parent's failure to sign off. It may take a few phone calls home to get this method firmly established.

Unfortunately positive reinforcement doesn't work for every child or in every situation. Another type of reinforcement that may be used is referred to as "negative reinforcement." "You can't do that (something you want to do) until you have done this (something you don't enjoy doing)" is an example of negative reinforcement. Its success is contingent upon being allowed to do what is desired as soon as the undesirable task is finished. Probably every teacher has kept children in at recess to complete work that should have already been finished. It works really well when the teacher uses it consistently. But if little Bobby gets away with unfinished work sometimes, it won't be as successful. This system is equally effective if the student is working to avoid an unpleasant situation such as detention or in-school suspension.

Human nature doesn't change. There have always been and always will be rebellious children. Even in the best classrooms and schools there will be occasions when that ugly word punishment must be used. In public schools, suspension is a favorite device, as well as alternate placement in a special class or school for discipline problems. Extra work may be required or removal of privileges may be used. Those students who participate in athletics may not be allowed to participate for a time. Some schools require delinquent students to come to school on Saturday. Schools may require that parents take disciplinary action. Some even require the parent to come to school and administer a spanking. In Kentucky, students who dropped out of school had their driver's license revoked.

As a last resort, schools have to be willing to take the ultimate punitive action, which is expulsion from the school. The law and public pressure have made this very difficult for public schools, but it still can be done. Christian schools understandably hesitate to take such action for fear they will be removing the child from Christian influence. However, if the child has been shown respect and love during her tenure in the school and all other avenues of discipline have been exhausted, it is unfair to everyone involved not to expel the trouble maker.

The Bible refers to such individuals as mockers and

scorners. A mocker is one who laughs at correction, and a scorner in Scripture is one who mocks at sin and at God's judgment of it. Christians forget that God's mercy will eventually be removed. Genesis 6:3 quotes the Lord, "My Spirit will not contend with man forever." The Bible also says through Soloman that, "A man who remains stiff-necked after many rebukes will suddenly be destroyed without remedy" (Proverbs 29:1).

Part of our problem with discipline is that we no longer accept that God's judgment will one day fall on unbelievers. The Lord has called parents and teachers to take every action necessary to discipline their children in time to avoid the judgment that is "without remedy." One other reason for expelling a rebellious and un-teachable student is that others learn from it. Not only that, but Proverbs 22:10 tells us, "Drive out the mocker, and out goes strife; quarrels and insults are ended." Every teacher has had a student that keeps things in a constant uproar. Arguments, fights, class disruption, and chaos follow him wherever he is.

One tremendous advantage that Christian schools have over public schools is the freedom to teach students the basis for discipline. God has placed parents and teachers in authority. There are numerous Scriptures concerning the need to be in submission to authority. The Bible teaches that God is orderly and deliberate in his actions, and that He has revealed his character through both the written and Living Word. In Christian schools, children can be taught that God's son, Jesus Christ, was obedient even to death, and that he never failed even in one point of the law. Students see that self-discipline is a fruit of the Spirit. They see that

Christ showed mercy to those who failed in their actions and offered forgiveness, so they are given hope when they fail.

One of the best ways for parents or teachers to minimize problems in discipline is to have reasonable expectations and to make sure that children are aware of and understand what is expected of them. Those in authority must then be very consistent in those expectations. There should be certain consequences for failure to comply, and this should be made known in advance.

In the classroom, teachers can avoid many problems simply by being organized, well-prepared and enthusiastic. They should be aware of what is going on at all times and keep activities moving along quickly from one thing to another, leaving no time in between for trouble to start. They need to handle any disruptions quickly and confidently with a minimum of lost time. Obviously it helps for the teacher to be rested and in good health, as a great deal of energy is required to constantly be on top of every situation and still be pleasant and friendly with a good sense of humor. It also helps to have an already prepared curriculum. A teacher who has to design his own curriculum will have to unnecessarily re-invent the wheel. A great deal of time and effort must be spent in deciding what to teach, in what order, and with what materials. When this is the case, materials needed must be gathered instead of having materials already prepared to order. A teacher has very little time and energy left to deal with students' other needs.

Other variables that cause a great deal of stress and confusion to parents and teachers in discipline are the conditions known as attention deficit disorder and hyperactivity. Children with these problems are much more challenging. Their stress and tolerance levels are different. Many books have been written to deal with these problems, and there is not space here to address these adequately. However, having been a teacher of many such students and the parent of one, I have found that most of the principles discussed in this chapter work for troubled children too.

One important thing to remember is the necessity of removing as much of the stress from physiological limitations as possible. Some stress reduction may need to be achieved through appropriate medication, diet, and rest. Other changes may need to be made in the physical environment around the child, and by adjusting expectations to fit the ability. Most of these children respond well to order and structure, and they like to know where the boundaries are. They do not adapt well to changes, so letting them know in advance that something is going to change and instituting changes gradually is helpful.

Teaching children is one of the most difficult jobs on earth. Christian parents ought to pray for the physical, mental, and spiritual health of their child's teacher. They should teach their children the basis for discipline by sharing the Scriptures concerning submission to authority and the example set by Jesus. They should model that attitude before their children and help them to recognize that self-discipline is a fruit of the Holy Spirit. Unfortunately even many of the children attending Christian schools do not get this kind of teaching at home. Therefore, it is very important for Christian teachers to share with students this biblical basis for authority and to model the right attitude of submission themselves. Children also need to know that God offers forgiveness and hope to those who seek it when they have failed. Christian teachers in public schools who cannot share from the Bible can model God's grace when they correct students in an attitude of love that does not excuse misbehavior, but is always ready to start over with a clean slate after the discipline is applied.

The emotional condition of the students in today's classrooms is far worse than those in the early seventies. Though divorce was already common at that time, now it is much more so. Children born to unwed mothers, those living in single parent homes, or in blended families are far more common in some classes than are children living with both biological parents. Shockingly, this is even the case in many Christian schools. It is most likely that the skyrocketing incidence of hyperactivity, attention deficit, behavior disorders, emotional disturbance, violence, and even suicide among children may in far too many cases be linked to this breakdown in the family.

Most schools, public and Christian, now have some form of before and after school programs for children. It is amazing to see the numbers of children who are dropped off as early as six thirty in the morning and picked up as late as possible, spending ten or eleven hours in the school's care. When they do get home, they may typically spend very little time with their exhausted parents. This absence of home and family support are enough to undermine a child's sense of security.

While parents are too inaccessible, today's children are

inundated with electronic babysitters. Televisions, DVDs, computers, video games, CD players, and the like are often unsupervised by parents. Some children have these in their bedrooms and stay up using them well after their parents are asleep. (Hyperactive children are often poor sleepers.) The raunchiness of the content children are getting through these is well known. Even basic cable television makes viewing full adult nudity and simulated sexual intercourse possible by just innocently flipping across the channels. Too many children are sleep deprived, overly stimulated, depressed, angry, confused, and emotionally starved. Is it any wonder that we are seeing an escalation of extreme discipline problems in our schools and throughout our culture?

Because parents work long hours and are overly stressed themselves, fast food is about all many kids get to eat, except on weekends if they are lucky. Children are overweight and under-nourished. Possibly some of the hyperactivity and attention problems seen by teachers can be attributed in part to diet and lack of sleep. It is well-known that sleep deprivation can lead to depression, and the old saying, "you are what you eat," may have some merit to it. However, compared to the emotional trauma many children are being subjected to from abusive parents, this may be the least of their problems. Lax discipline and overindulgence of their children by some parents wanting to soothe their sense of guilt for being absent is also a form of child abuse.

Children often witness violent confrontations between family members, the effects of drug addiction, alcoholism, and extramarital affairs. Far too many are verbally, physically, or sexually abused. They are confused about relationships and are abnormally fearful. Furthermore, they pass on the verbal and physical abuse to others around them. Children treat each other with cruelty and disrespect, not because of being disciplined, but often because of the lack of it. Bullying is a problem almost universally in today's schools.

Many parents refuse to expend the time or the effort to set and enforce disciplinary boundaries for their children, and will not allow the school to discipline them. Many already feel guilty because they instinctively realize their children are missing something important, but they either don't know how or don't feel they can do anything about it. The "experts" have led them to believe that all they have to do is give their children enough love and everything will turn out all right. The problem is that they have been given a warped sense of just what constitutes love. The Bible makes clear that the one who loves his child will discipline him (Proverbs 13:24). Many Christians believe that means even to spank when needed. Now the government is trying to tell parents they can't do this. The government (because Christians have been ineffective in their influence) has also done everything possible to prevent children from being given an education grounded in the truth.

What has happened to the religious training of children during this time is most disturbing of all. Even in many Christian schools, as many as half of the students are un-churched. This says that those parents are depending on the school to take care of all of the child's spiritual training. What a false sense of security! What children see lived out at home will likely have a far greater impact on them than what they hear at school. And, the unfortunate truth is that even some "Christian" schools may fail to put a priority on teaching children biblical truth. For some, a short chapel once a week is all the religious training given. Even for those schools who want to make teaching biblical principles a priority, there may be teachers who fail to see its importance and therefore give it little place in the day's activities. Some Christian teachers are in the dark about the importance of a worldview that is consistent with the Bible. They don't recognize the influence of secularism on many curriculums and textbooks they are using and even in their own ways of looking at the world. They (we) are all victims of our own secular education.

Christian schools that have made Bible teaching a priority in the curriculum are to be commended. It is important to foster an attitude of respect for God's truth. It might be easier to do this if Bible classes are taught differently from the rest of the curriculum. Bible class should not be just another class with similar academic expectations. This class should definitely be the most enjoyable class of the day.

"Choose for yourselves this day whom you will serve....But as for me and my household, we will serve the LORD."

(Joshua 24:15)

CHOOSING TRUTH IN A WORLDVIEW

What difference does our belief system make?

One of the most important decisions a parent will ever make is how and where to have his child educated. Education is the training of the mind, and it will determine to a great extent how the child thinks. It will have a tremendous impact on what he will become. Every system of education is built on some philosophical foundation, and every philosophy has behind it some theology. David A. Noebel, in his book *Understanding the Times,* stated that "all worldviews contain a theology—that is, all begin with a religious declaration" (1). He describes worldview as everything we believe that impacts our "understanding of God, the world, and man's relations to God and the world" (2). Those who constantly yelp about separation of church and state in education are either ignorant of the existence and power of worldviews, or they are hiding an agenda that is very dangerous to our society.

Francis Schaeffer contended that worldview affects every facet of a society and that everything that has changed about American life can be traced back to the failure of Christians to apply biblical truth to every issue in life. We have allowed secularists to apply the humanist worldview to public life, and we are reaping the consequences through the breakdown of morality and virtue. We mistakenly thought we could allow them access to the minds of our children without mortal harm. Noebel, in *Understanding the Times,* cited a U.S. News and World Report article that claimed American campuses have at least ten thousand Marxist professors. Those professors cannot just believe in Marx's economic theories without accepting his entire worldview, which rests on atheism. Even though much of Marxism concerning economics has been proved fatally wrong before the watching world, the philosophy lives on in American universities. It is still influencing policy decisions in education, law, and government.

As has already been stated, the worldview that has dominated the public school arena for the past generation is humanism. Atheism is its theological foundation. According to Noebel, the *Humanist Manifesto I* "described the universe as 'self-existing and not created'…and declared, 'The time has passed for theism.'…" (3). Major players in the history of public education, such as John Dewey, embraced the ideas in the *Humanist Manifesto.* In fact, Dewey was one of the signers. Most people educated in the public schools of this country are acquainted with the role of evolution in our schools. Die-hard evolutionists don't mind confessing that there is no place for God in their theory. However, the humanists' goal for the world has made it necessary to cloak their ideas in terms that would be more acceptable to the majority. Educators (meaning primarily those at the top who make the decisions for the direction of the schools) have for the most part been successful in convincing people that evolution and religion can go together. However, they cannot fit together, for true humanism has disavowed God and has as its newfound theology the supremacy of man. It must not be forgotten that humanism gave birth to the theory of evolution.

Everything taught through the public schools in recent years has been touched in some way by the philosophy of humanism and its accompanying theology. It impacts our ideas about history, biology, sociology, economics, law, psychology, politics, and ethics. For Christians anything that denies God as author and sustainer of life, that says we determine our own destinies with no need for God, should be firmly rejected. We should denounce any idea that truth evolves and needs to be revised to agree with so-called science. We ought to especially reject having such ideas determine the direction of education for our children. However, it would appear that the only hope for a return to education based on knowledge of the truth is for parents to exercise choice. At the present time this has been made extremely difficult because of the tremendous cost of education. While many parents are beginning to choose Christian schools or home schools, many more haven't yet understood the importance of such or cannot see a way to make it happen. Any discussion of choice in education raises tempers and blood pressures everywhere and is so politically charged that it's hard to get good information.

Stephen Arons, in his book *A Short Route to Chaos,* proposed that Americans consider an amendment to the Constitution that would guarantee all parents the right to choice in education. Surely the need for choice is greater now than at any other time in our history. It may even be necessary if we are to maintain freedom from excessive governmental control over our families and possibly could even affect whether we are to remain free as a nation. However, the issue of choice in education is something that Americans are sharply divided on. And a legitimate question is, how could government be kept out of the operation of schools even if parents could choose which one to send their children to? One of the biggest problems in the minds of many people concerning the issue of choice is the separation of church and state. Taxpayers recoil from the idea of funding religious instruction with which they do not agree. However, shouldn't we be equally as concerned about funding so many unwholesome government-sanctioned ideologies masquerading as truth? Then there is the question of who is going to keep watch on all these schools to see that they are actually teaching children anything of benefit, if not the government. A look at the evidence of how private schools are doing as compared to public schools would be a good place to start. After all, private school students take college entrance exams at probably higher percentages than others. Also, analyses of NAEP (National Assessment of Education Progress) results from the Department of Education itself show that "students reading achievement is substantially higher in private schools than in public schools" (4). Strikingly, this report also showed that "...students who seem to benefit most from a private education are those whose parents are at lower educational levels, suggesting that private education is helping to expand access to equal educational opportunities" (5). A question that doesn't get much attention is, are there alternative ways to even out the financial field for private schools without directly using tax dollars and thus risking government intervention? One possible idea might be to allow some tax breaks for individuals and companies who donate funds for private education. Especially fitting would be tax breaks to those who would provide scholarships for needy students to attend private schools of their choice.

The State of Wisconsin won Supreme Court approval for a voucher program in which the state essentially gave money to the parents to use at the school of their choice. The checks were sent to the institution chosen by the parents who then endorsed the checks. The court did not allow the state to become involved in any way with the school's governance, curriculum, or day-to-day affairs. Opponents to choice will continue to scream and throw tantrums about the "destruction of the public schools and the funneling of tax money into religious schools" (6). It is curious that these same people seldom mention that tax dollars have been going to students who choose religiously affiliated colleges for many years. There has been no evidence of the destruction of public universities that would resemble the predictions for public elementary through high schools in a choice environment. Perhaps that is because humanists believe that if they are given free access to children's minds for the first thirteen years of schooling, most of them will choose public universities anyway. Even if they don't, the die has been cast, and the philosophers don't expect many children to escape from the education they have already received. Also, they are aware, even if most Christians aren't, that humanistic philosophies have made their way into many of the Christian universities as well.

President Clinton vetoed legislation to fund tax benefits for parents who send their children to private schools, saying he opposed it because it would help richer families while doing "virtually nothing for average families" (7). The president himself proposed twelve billion dollars to build schools, hire teachers, and expand after-school programs for public schools. In the spring of 2000, President Clinton called on Congress to vote two hundred fifty million new tax dollars to fix failing schools or shut them down and let students transfer to a better public school. Republicans pushed for allowing students to transfer to private or parochial schools with the aid of education savings accounts, but the president promised to veto anything other than help for public schools. The president's insistence that vouchers do nothing for underprivileged children rings hollow when one takes an unbiased look at what is happening in Wisconsin. The program there targeted low-income students for aid to attend private schools, and, as already stated, tests results show that these children make more progress.

There will probably be more legal hurdles for the Wisconsin plan, but the court's decision to allow it to go forward is a refreshing turn of events for those concerned about the current state of public education. Other states have had their choice programs thrown out by the courts because of conflicts with their state constitutions. However, the idea of choice is gaining momentum across the nation, and there will no doubt be other states that will eventually succeed in bringing it to their citizens.

Most rational people can at least agree that the private sector usually does a better job for the dollar in almost any endeavor than the government can do because of the endless complexities of bureaucratic red tape. It has been estimated that public schools employ about thirty times the number of administrators per pupil as private schools. After all, administrators are expected to be change agents for the schools, and they must somehow justify their existence. They do this by devising one program after another to implement, while private schools can quietly go about the business of educating students.

The naysayers on the issue of school choice always raise the objection that no matter how you allocate the tax dollars to parochial schools, it is still going toward "proselytizing and conversion of students." (8) Whoa! What they are really saying is that it's all right to use tax dollars to indoctrinate students against their parents' beliefs as long as it is publicly sanctioned indoctrination. They say this is okay because that's what the constitution calls for. While the Constitution does not allow government to get entangled in religion or to sanction one religion above others, it certainly does not forbid parents to sanction a particular religion. The Wisconsin Supreme Court ruled that as long as the state gives funds to parents equally, whether for public, private, or sectarian schools on a nondiscriminatory basis, it does not violate the Constitution. In part the decision said,

A policeman protects a catholic, not because he is a catholic; it is because he is a member of our society. The fireman protects the church school, but not because it is a church school; it is because it is property, part of the assets of our society. Neither the fireman nor the policeman has to ask before he renders aid, "Is this man or building identified with the church?" (9)

The judge writing this opinion said, "The benefit neither promotes religion nor is hostile to it." (10) That makes sense. Parents who fear their children might be proselytized have other choices of where to send them. In a truly democratic system of schooling, there would be many choices of schools available—something for everyone. The choice opponents are aware of this. What they usually don't come out and say publicly is that they don't believe parents can be trusted to make wise choices for their children's education, and they want to remove any hint of Christianity from all education.

Another point opponents bring up is that parochial schools have the opportunity to throw out disruptive students and public schools don't. While it may be more difficult to get rid of disruptive students, it is not impossible for public schools to expel them. If it isn't being done, it's because legislators and school officials do not have enough backbone to do it. Parents with children in public schools must fight a firmly entrenched political system to assure that their children have a safe and uninterrupted learning environment. The situation is not likely to change until public schools start losing students and the money that comes with them. For those who predict the demise of public education with the advent of choice programs, one should rightly wonder how much confidence these people really have in the schools' ability to change what it is that dissatisfies parents. Healthy competition usually results in changes for the better.

In answer to the charge that choice programs would hurt disabled students, the truth is that many parents of disabled students already choose private education over the public schools. There are even many private schools that have opened for the very purpose of serving these children. Parents who place children in these programs must certainly have confidence in the schools or they wouldn't keep their children there.

Many of the students being drawn to private and Christian schools are those who have been labeled by the school system with Attention Deficit Disorder or hyperactivity (which includes ADD). Others have not been tested for these disorders, but their parents have gotten messages from the schools that their children have a problem.

Every public schoolteacher is familiar with the jump in numbers of kids on medication for hyperactivity. Some estimates have placed it as high as fifteen percent of boys in some school districts. The percentage appears to be higher in the elementary grades. In my first year of teaching at a new Christian school, thirty-two percent of my class had been labeled as hyperactive, Attention Deficit, or learning disabled, though not all were being medicated for it. Some schools estimate that close to forty percent of students have been labeled as ADD, but most are not receiving medication.

The results of a study released in the spring of 2000 showed that the use of stimulants among two- to four-year-olds in some parts of the country had doubled or even tripled between 1991 and 1995. (11) There doesn't seem to be any question that something is wrong. No one seems to know whether something is wrong with our children, wrong with our expectations, or wrong with our society to cause such a rise in use of drugs to control the behavior of children.

As already discussed in an earlier chapter, not all children labeled as such are really learning disabled. Such is probably the case as well for many thought to have Attention Deficit Disorder. Some hyperactive children may just be lacking discipline. Diet, sleep deprivation, and excessive use of video games, or inappropriate visual images through computer or television may also contribute. Parents who have lost control over their children for whatever reason usually feel some guilt. They often try to fix the problem by moving the child from school to school. Sometimes they are fortunate enough to find a school, either private or public, where real help is found.

No doubt there are many complex contributing factors involved in the problems parents face in raising their children. One of the most basic is the worldview espoused by the parents, by their schools, and even by their churches. Christian parents must first determine that they are getting the truth. The only way to know if church leaders are firmly grounded in Scriptural truth is to study the Bible continuously with a reliance on the Holy Spirit for revelation. It is only then that parents can begin to accurately assess the worldviews around them and make wise choices regarding their children's education.

Regardless of what type of school a child is enrolled in, it is the Christian parent's job to pray daily for their child, for his friends, and especially for his teachers and other authorities who make decisions that will impact their child's education. "Mom's In Touch" is a wonderful ministry for any mother desiring to know more about how to impact the schools through prayer. These ladies meet on a regular basis to pray for their children, their schools, the teachers and staff, as well as for each other. They believe that united prayer is powerful and effective, and they have seen miraculous answers. The organization gives suggestions for how to pray as well as ideas for how to minister to the teachers and staff in tangible ways.

Parents who have children in public schools need to know what is going on in their child's classroom, in local schoolboard meetings, and what decisions are being made at the state level. Focus On the Family works with individual states to help them set up a system for notifying subscribers to their *Citizen* magazine about state politics, especially those affecting the family. It might be a good idea to subscribe to this and read it regularly. Parents should get involved, and when legislators are looking for input on bills before them, let their voices be heard. Also, parents ought to know what religious rights their child has in the school. The following are among those rights:

1. the right to pray individually or in groups, or to discuss religious views with peers

2. the right to express their religious beliefs in the form of reports, homework, and artwork

3. the right to meet in religious clubs in secondary schools on the same basis as other clubs

4. the right to student-initiated prayer at school activities

5. the right to learn about religion as long as no religion is promoted or school endorsed

Above all else, Christian parents must be sure their children are being immersed in the Scriptures on a daily basis at home, not just at church. They need to make sure their children are talking to them about what goes on at school. Children must be taught that everything they hear, read, and view should be compared to the Scriptures to see if there is any truth in them. They should be made aware that teachers can be wrong sometimes, and that not everything written in books is true.

In looking for a Christian school, parents must discern the school's philosophies. Do they accept the Bible as the authority for all life issues? Is their Scriptural understanding sound? Do they believe that every human being has been created in the image of God and for the purpose of fellowship with Him, that each person has a spirit that will go on living eternally somewhere, and that every individual is accountable to God for the deeds done in the body? Do they accept the sacrificial death, burial, and resurrection of Jesus Christ as historically true and essential to salvation? Do they see their primary goal as the leading of every child to a saving faith in Jesus Christ? Do they believe that all subject areas can be taught best from a truly Christian perspective, and are they committed to equipping students with the truth so that they might develop a distinctly Christian mindset and lifestyle? Do they have high academic standards as well as excellent discipline? What type of curriculum do they use? Do they have orderly classroom environments that are open to creativity and improvement? How well trained are their teachers? Have they received training specifically for Christian education? Is the school accredited, and if not, do they have a definite plan for getting to that point? How often do they hold chapel for students, and how are leaders recruited? Do the teachers have daily or weekly devotions together?

If there is not a suitable Christian school available, parents might want to consider home schooling. The home school movement is rapidly growing, and there are many supports available. Some Christian school curriculums are available to parents who want to use them at home. Most Christian schools can put parents in contact with either another home school parent or give addresses of publishers of Christian curriculums. Home-schooled students may even arrange to take achievement tests with the appropriate class in a Christian school.

It is my personal belief after three decades of involvement in education that there is little hope for change in the current public school situation regarding Christian values. We will not be able to take back our country through the public schools, at least not at this time. I believe that it is God's will to use Christian education as well as Christian media as a part of reviving the nation. Schools where God is allowed to work freely in changing individuals and families will in time change communities. It will affect our churches and how we respond to the needs of those around us. It will have an impact on what we expect from our leaders and who we elect as well as on the decisions they will make.

The time has come for every Christian parent in America to assess our society with a critical eye and especially our schools in view of their tremendous impact on that society. Critical questions that need to be asked are: What are my goals in raising my own children? What do I expect from my children's education? Can I trust the schools with my child's whole development? Are public schools headed in the right direction? Are they helping or hindering our society? Is it possible to fix them? What does God expect from me as a parent?

Regardless of a parent's personal answers to the questions above, every reader needs to take a stand regarding the growth of Christian education in this country. Is there a need for it? Should it be a protected right for parents to choose their children's education? If the answers to these questions are affirmative, the following questions would be: How can I help to defend and protect Christian education? Should I help financially? Do I have talents that could be put to use on a volunteer basis?

It is my hope and prayer that these pages will encourage some real critical thinking and action from Christian parents, grandparents, and other concerned citizens. The future of this nation depends on whether or not we will return to a Christian worldview. William Penn said, "If we are not governed by God, then we will be ruled by tyrants." (12) John

Witherspoon, signer of the Declaration of Independence, said, "He is the best friend of American liberty who is most sincere and active in promoting pure and undefiled religion." (13) History has born out the truth of these statements. The question now is whether Christians will be willing to take the action necessary to reverse the tide of destructive forces waging war on our culture.

"Buy the truth and do not sell it; get wisdom, discipline and understanding."

(Proverbs 23:23)

TRAMPLING ON TRUTH

What lies led to a crippled America?

America has to a great extent given up on and lost touch with the concept of truth. The word is often used in our society, but its meaning has lost any real significance. As already stated, it all came about through a total shift in worldview from one of biblical Christianity to one of humanism. The deception about the nature of truth has been spread throughout the culture by way of public education, the media, and the courts. Among the top enemies of truth that humanistic thinking has brought us are: the theory of evolution; the Kinsey Report, leading to acceptance of homosexuality; abortion (with a growing disrespect for human life at all levels); and no-fault divorce.

One of the biggest frauds of all time has been the theory of evolution, which may have done more to advance other deceptions than anything else could have. Regardless of what some proponents may say, it is the atheistic foundation for most of the worldviews that stand in opposition to truth. Its appearance was intended to nullify the belief in God, the Bible, and creation. Leading evolution scientist Richard Dawkins admitted that Darwin made it possible to be an "intellectually fulfilled atheist." True neo-Darwinists allow no room for the creation viewpoint. In fact, they disallow the supernatural at all. They believe that the universe and everything in it were a result of mere chance and that all life evolved from a common ancestor that resulted from purely random forces of nature.

From the outset of Darwin's assertions, credible scientists found the so-called evidence to be faulty. However, sold-out believers in evolution have consistently referred to ten different proofs that they purport to be the unquestionable evidence. Biologist Jonathan Wells calls these the "icons of evolution." In his book that bears that title, Dr. Wells presented a large body of evidence that casts serious doubt on every one of them. Wells said, "Darwinism encourages distortion of the truth." (1) He quotes Constance Holden, who wrote in a 1981 article for *Science,* "The primary scientific evidence is a pitifully small array of bones from which to construct man's evolutionary history." (2) He also credits Henry Gee, chief science writer for *Nature,* with the claim that "all the evidence for human evolution 'between about ten and five millions years ago—several thousand generations of living creatures—can be fitted into a small box.'" (3) Wells went on to quote Ian Tattersall, American Museum of Natural History curator, in a 1996 statement: "In paleoanthropology, the patterns we perceive are as likely to result from our unconscious mindsets as from the evidence itself." (4) Of course, the mindset of many scientists in America is that the fact of evolution is unquestionable.

Among the ten icons of evolution, perhaps one of the most blatantly falsified is the oft-used drawings of vertebrate embryos produced by German biologist Ernst Haeckel. It is now widely recognized among biologists and especially embryologists that the drawings distorted the truth. Haeckel selected certain embryos that he could manipulate to fit his theory that similarities in embryos at the earliest stages proved a common ancestor. Dr. Wells, who is himself an embryologist with two Ph.D.s, criticized Haeckel for not only distorting the embryos in his pictures but also for omitting earlier stages in which the embryos look very different from each other. According to Wells, Haeckel was criticized heavily by his contemporaries and often called a fraud. (5) Nevertheless, his drawings still show up unchanged in biology textbooks.

A second icon known as the Miller-Urey Experiment purported to prove that the building blocks of life could be created in a laboratory by simulating the early conditions of earth's atmosphere. Among other problems with the theory, many scientists (particularly geo-scientists) now recognize that there is a good bit of evidence that Earth's early atmosphere was not at all like what the two scientists claimed and could not have produced the first cell as they implied. Neo-Darwinists, however, refuse to admit the mounting evidence and dismiss it as impossible because it would be contrary to their argument. They contend that since it is a given that life evolved spontaneously, the early atmosphere had to be the way they believe it was. This is not only getting the cart before the horse, it is totally unscientific. Again, this experiment continues to be stubbornly held up as evidence for evolution, despite many questions from scientists themselves.

Another widely publicized example that evolutionists use is the peppered moth study in which large numbers of dark-colored moths in Britain began to replace the typical light-colored ones during the industrial revolution. Bernard Kettlewell performed some experiments that appeared to prove that natural selection in moths had occurred when tree trunks became darkened by pollution. His pictures continue to be a favorite in biology textbooks, even though it is now known that the pictures were staged. Since peppered moths do not actually rest on tree trunks, moths were glued to the trees. Kettlewell's other experiments involved placing live moths on the trunks of trees where they tended to stay because they do not move much in the daylight. Neo-Darwinists who use this example usually fail to tell students about the reversal of the dark-colored trend among moths that took place a few years later. They also fail to mention that the phenomenon of an increase in dark-colored moths also took place in a part of Britain that had relatively little industrial pollution.

There are similar discrepancies in the evidence given for the remaining icons. Furthermore, some exhibits, such as "Piltdown Man" and "Archaeoraptor" (a fossil that supposedly had the forelimbs of a bird and the tail of a dinosaur) remained in museums for decades before being exposed as the forgeries they really were. Nevertheless, neo-Darwinists continue to claim that the evidence for evolution is unquestionable.

The truth is that evolutionists cannot afford to have their beloved theory scrutinized because their entire paradigm rests upon it. Evolution in reality is more philosophy than true science, and the secular humanists it has produced have staked everything on it. Many really do believe the entire cosmos created itself and that man is a mere accident in time. They believe it because they want to believe it. Genesis 1:1 says, "In the beginning God created the heavens and the earth." John 1:3 says it this way: "Through him all things were made; without him nothing was made that has been made." Using evolution as their proof text, progressives believe the Bible is totally fabricated and based on mere human superstition. Their need to believe in Darwin's theory forces them to ignore or try to silence any conflicting evidence.

Another great deception of the past century was the so-called research done by Alfred Kinsey with the blessing of a prestigious university and plenty of tax dollars to pay for it. Kinsey and his cohorts in crime used children as young as infants for sexual experimentation, manipulation, and abuse. Then they proceeded to publish reports that humans are sexually stimulated from birth and that homosexuality is an inborn characteristic in about ten percent of all people. Their intention was to legitimize sexual perversion. No doubt Kinsey and his group knew that both the Old and New Testaments forbid homosexuality. The book of Leviticus calls it a *detestable* practice, and Paul in the book of Romans tells how God gave wicked people over in their sinful desires to sexual impurity. He makes it even clearer by describing those desires: "Even their women exchanged natural relations for unnatural ones. In the same way the men also abandoned natural relations with women and were inflamed with lust for one another. Men committed *indecent* acts with other men, and received in themselves the due penalty for their *perversion*" (Romans 1:26–27). The Bible refers to the practice of homosexuality as detestable, indecent, and perverse. From these verses, it isn't difficult to see why sexual perverts want to discredit or rewrite the Bible or at least persuade themselves and others that not all of it can be taken seriously as the Word of God.

The so-called right to abortion was an inevitable result of the sexual revolution and the growing humanistic thinking. Women were told that a fetus is just a blob of tissues, and they could get rid of it without any need for remorse. They were led to believe that life in the womb is not fully human. They were even convinced that a fetus cannot feel pain. In the Psalms David wrote, "For you created my inmost being; you knit me together in my mother's womb. I praise you because I am fearfully and wonderfully made" (Psalms 139:13). He continues, "Your eyes saw my unformed body. All the days ordained for me were written in your book before one of them came to be" (Psalms 139:16). In the New Testament, the Bible describes how John the Baptist leaped for joy in his mother's womb when the voice of the Virgin Mary was heard (Luke 1:44). Luke, a physician and historian, may well have gotten these words from Mary herself, for her cousin Elizabeth described to her how she was filled with the Holy Spirit when the child within her reacted to Mary's voice. Both Mary and Elizabeth knew they were carrying sons because of the advance announcement through angels. They also knew that God had very special plans for their sons. Only a rejection of God's Word could lead one to conclude that God does not care about those in the womb.

In the summer of 2006, legislators passed a bill that

would allow federal funding of the use of human embryos for research with stem cells. When President Bush vetoed the bill, he was surrounded by young children who had been adopted as embryos from fertility clinics. These so-called "snowflake" babies were to be a reminder that human embryos are not just "spare parts" but human beings. Of course, many people in this age of abortion cannot make that connection, and President Bush has been heavily criticized for not caring about all the people who might be helped by stem cell research. One man put the issue into stark perspective. Though he was confined to life in a wheelchair, he pointed to his adopted "snowflake" children and said that he would not want a cure for himself that could only come at the expense of the lives of his children. Currently there is no evidence of any cure coming from fetal stem cells. However, there have been encouraging signs that stem cells retrieved from other means such as from umbilical cords or adult stem cells may prove greatly beneficial. These do not receive the same measure of publicity as that involving embryos. Could this be the case because so many progressives want to protect abortion?

Another devastating force in this nation has been divorce, which is responsible for the destruction of multitudes of families. Its consequences have had an incalculable impact on our society, and it is as rampant among Christians as it is with unbelievers. Most of our society has come to accept it as normal and unavoidable in our time. Although it is certainly not an unpardonable sin, it is sin nonetheless. Jesus made that crystal clear when he said, "Anyone who divorces his wife and marries another woman commits adultery against her. And if she divorces her husband and marries another man, she commits adultery" (Mark 10:10–12). Malachi in the Old Testament wrote, "I hate divorce, says the Lord" (Malachi 2:16). The prophet even told the people of his time that God was no longer accepting their offerings because of their divorces (Malachi 2:13–14). God still takes divorce seriously even if our society no longer does.

Because of the falling away from Christian values experienced by this nation, we have been on a downward spiral for a long time. If there is no reversal of this trend, America will eventually self-destruct, as happened to other civilizations throughout history. The Bible says that unchecked wickedness (particularly sexual perversions) leads to a time when the land becomes defiled. Through Moses God told the people of Israel, "Even the land (of Canaan) was defiled; so I punished it for its sin, and the land vomited out its inhabitants" (Leviticus 18:24–25). This was followed by the stern warning,

> You must not do any of these detestable things, for
> all these things were done by the people who lived
> in the land before you, and the land became defiled.
> And if you defile the land, it will vomit you out as it
> vomited out the nations that were before you.
>
> (Leviticus 18:26–28)

In modern times one can travel to the ancient ruins of Ephesus to see the historical record of what happens to societies that become sold out to idol worship and sexual perversions. The site of the old temple to the goddess of fertility is now a disgusting swamp.

Christ's admonition was that Christians should be the salt and light of the earth. We are to live in a righteous manner as an example to those around us, and we are supposed to speak the truth that exposes the darkness. However, too often Christians are so immersed in the same destructive habits and attitudes of the culture that we are a part of the problem instead of the answer. To a great extent, we have lost our witness. Many Christians are not convinced that the Bible has the answers. They don't know the truth because they are biblically ignorant, and there is no power in their lives to positively impact a decaying society. The unfortunate truth is that many people who claim Christianity really don't know Christ. They cannot be Christians because the very name means "little Christ." Christians are those who believe Christ to be all he claimed to be and who obey his commands because they love Him. They have surrendered to his lordship over their lives. They believe he has revealed truth to us through the Bible and that his words will never pass away.

Another trampling of truth that is taking place with renewed vigor is the attempt to discredit the authenticity of the Bible. The blockbuster book and movie *The Da Vinci Code* makes the case that the New Testament is unreliable and that Jesus never claimed divinity. Among the author's accusations are several that are blatantly false. He claims that it was the emperor Constantine who chose what books to include in the biblical canon. No serious scholar would make this claim. The only council that met at that time was the Council of Nicea, and they did not even discuss the canon. It was already established by then. The New Testament was written within a relatively short period of time after the death of Jesus, and the authors were either eyewitnesses or contemporaries. Even the most liberal critics who have studied the evidence must admit that all of the New Testament books were written while many eyewitnesses were still alive. It is well documented that the Apostle Paul wrote the books attributed to him between AD fifty-five and sixty. On the other hand, the gnostic gospels, which Dan Brown claims were excluded by Constantine, were written two or three hundred years later by those who usurped the names of apostles and contemporaries of Jesus but had no credible knowledge at all.

The Da Vinci Code also claims that the Dead Sea Scrolls cast doubt on the New Testament. However, the scrolls only include Jewish writings which predate the birth of Christ. And, concerning the authenticity of the Old Testament, Jesus himself quoted often from them as authoritative. He said about them that, "These are the Scriptures that testify about me" (John 5:39). He also stated that, "The Scripture cannot be broken" (John 10:35). In spite of what people like Dan Brown say, there is overwhelming evidence for the authenticity of the Bible, including the number of surviving manuscripts, the accuracy of these, the closeness of their writing to the time of the events, and the archaeological proof of the historical accuracy.

Another accusation made in Brown's work was that Jesus did not claim divinity and that the early church did not make the claim. This is blatantly in disagreement with the four Gospels and the writings of Paul. Brown makes the preposterous assertion that Constantine pressured the bishops at the Council of Nicea to vote on the question of Christ's divinity, and that only by a close vote was it established. The truth according to historical records is that only two of the over two hundred bishops failed to sign the creed. The creed did not establish the claim of Christ's divinity, for that was already believed by the Christian church. It was to settle the fact that the church believed that Jesus was one with God the Father from eternity and not another created "God."

Brown further tries to discredit Jesus as Lord by making the claim that he was a mere mortal who was married to Mary Magdalene. He has absolutely no historical evidence for the claim and tries to pin the whole assertion on Leonardo Da Vinci, who lived fifteen hundred years after Christ and had no authoritative credibility whatsoever. *The Da Vinci Code* is just another smear tactic to try to discredit Christianity. It will no doubt confuse a lot of people and cause many to doubt. However, there have been similar schemes throughout the ages, and this too will fade away.

It is crucial for Christians to develop in our children a distinctly Bible-centered Christian view of life and a lifestyle consistent with that view if we are to be a positive influence on our society. However, it is becoming increasingly clear that for most of us, this objective cannot be realized in the context of public schooling at this time. It is inevitable that compulsory education funded by government money will be politicized, and those factions that have the most political clout will succeed in force-feeding their ideas to the next generation through the public schools.

Educators have been trained to accept the educational philosophies of humanistic thinkers. Most probably do not have a complete picture of where those ideas came from and how they contradict biblical truth. We must remember that many of the framers of current public education philosophy had rejected the tenets of the Christian faith. They rejected the authority of the Bible and adhered to faith in the basic goodness of mankind. Many really believed that education was all that was needed to create the perfect society. In their eyes any belief is as good as any other if it works. Therefore one of the major goals of public education is to promote tolerance for all beliefs, ideas, attitudes, and lifestyles (with the only exception being biblical Christianity). To be critical of any other beliefs is now considered intolerant, bigoted, and mean-spirited. In fact, it is thought to be so bad that it should be made a crime, while any other speech, no matter how vile, is supposed to be constitutionally protected. It would appear that infecting our children with tolerance is far more important to some in education than teaching them to become critical thinkers.

Dr. James Dobson, in his June 1998 Focus on the Family Newsletter, reported on a "hate crimes" conference hosted by the White House and the president in which Bill Clinton told a group of participants that "public schools across the nation should institute pro-homosexual diversity programs to 'teach (children) a different way.'" Dr. Dobson's letter was a warning to Christians about the well-funded pro-homosexual agenda for teaching their lifestyle to elementary school children as well as gaining control over high school and college curricula.

In March of 2004, the Family Research Council posted a story on their Web site about an explicit sex education pamphlet being used by Planned Parenthood through the Girl Scouts to teach girls as young as ten about sex, masturbation, and birth control. If not addressed in that particular pamphlet, Planned Parenthood will sooner or later get around to educating these young girls on the legitimacy of homosexuality.

In an article for the January 27, 2000, *Louisville Courier-Journal,* syndicated writer Mona Charen accused gays of manipulating public opinion "with the help of an obliging press." (6) She claimed that "the Vermont Supreme Court has now branded the preference for heterosexual unions enshrined in the laws of fifty states to be mere bigotry." (7) One of the most troubling points of her article was the formation of an alliance of education groups and psychological associations to distribute booklets to all public school districts throughout the nation. These booklets would urge schools to "create a safe and healthy environment" for the homosexual students. These are blatant attempts to use public education to create an environment not of mere tolerance but one of affirmation of the homosexual lifestyle. In the summer of 2006, it was reported by a Christian organization that the Environmental Protection Agency, using American tax dollars, had declared June to be gay and lesbian pride month and publicly advocated that homosexuality should not only be tolerated but be embraced as a lifestyle. Charen's article and others since then have been reminders of how the courts and the media have become a vehicle for spreading humanistic thinking across the nation. This type of thinking leads inevitably to an unwholesome change in our culture that will eventually destroy us if unchecked.

This moral breakdown has been creeping into our society little by little since the sexual revolution of the sixties. In truth, its advance began long before that when humanists got their stranglehold on the public schools. We as a nation have been scarcely aware of what was happening. Francis Schaeffer lamented the fact that Christians in all professions including theology, education, and law failed to sound the alarm when the assault began. We have been like the proverbial frog in the kettle who is content while the heat is gradually and imperceptibly raising the temperature of the water around us to boiling. Someone needs to yell, "Jump!" so loudly that we can't miss it.

Some estimates have placed up to eighty-eight percent of America's youth among the unchurched. A recent Barna poll showed only thirty-four percent of Generation X claiming to be "absolutely committed to the Christian faith," while fifty-two percent of baby boomers and seventy percent of seniors over the age of seventy-four claimed such a commitment. (8) The research went on to show that only thirty-seven percent of all those polled had read the Bible outside church in the last week. Gallup polls have found that Bible reading has declined from seventy-three percent in the 1980s to around fifty-nine percent in 2006. However, those who claim frequent readership of the Bible has dropped to thirty-seven percent. Gallup also found that those most likely to read the Bible are women, nonwhites, and older people. He found higher readership among Republicans and political conservatives. (9) Similar studies have indicated that there may be a correlation between level of education and Bible reading, with those having post-graduate degrees being less likely to be regular readers. These statistics do not show that smarter or more educated people reject truth because they have learned about the real evidence against it. There is no such evidence. Many brilliant and highly educated people have examined the evidence carefully and find that it supports biblical truth. What the statistics show is that there is a connection between education philosophies and the drift of our society away from faith in God and recognition of our dependence on Him.

It is imperative that God's people wake up. God has called all Christians to minister to the body of Christ. An important part of our ministry is to be faithful in supporting His plan for the family, which is of such great importance that He established it even before the church. One of the greatest challenges facing families is the education of their children.

God has raised up many Christian ministries in this generation to encourage, strengthen, and protect the family. For that we ought to be thankful and support these through our prayers and financial gifts. However, we also need to hold ministries accountable. We need to examine them, know where they stand in faithfulness to the truth, and how they use our gifts. Some Christian ministries may have handicapped themselves somewhat by a sort of snobbery toward those who have received their professional experience in the secular world. I detected it coming out of public school into Christian education. My husband, with close to thirty years of experience in secular radio and TV, encountered even more suspicion when he began to apply with Christian stations. This is not to say that everyone in the Christian organizations contacted had that attitude, but many did. It is somewhat understandable and no doubt results partly from the fear of allowing worldly influences to creep into the ministry through those who have worked in secular settings. There may, however, also be some jealousy involved and a subconscious desire to protect one's own turf. In other words, if I don't feel I'm better at something than you are, I can at least convince myself that I'm more righteous than you are. This is sinful pride. May God deliver us from it.

Christian ministries must be always vigilant that those in charge do not slip into the temptation to see it as "their" ministry and take an attitude of ownership. There is too often a tendency among Christians in leadership roles to begin to think that everything depends on them. Some of them (subconsciously, perhaps) believe that they alone can protect the ministry from outside corruption from "the world." They can't. "Unless the Lord builds the house, its builders labor in vain" (Psalm 127:1).

An openness to the truth must reveal that every Christian has come out of the world. Christ's disciples certainly did. I have been puzzled for years about the Scripture that states, "The people of this world are more shrewd in dealing with their own kind than are the people of light" (Luke 16:8). Admittedly, it may be taking it somewhat out of context, but one has to wonder if we Christians are sometimes guilty of being so heavenly minded that we are of no earthly good.

There is no justification for our rejecting the talents of other Christian people solely on the basis of prejudice. A look at history shows that God often has had to throw out the old institutions and make new vessels for "new wine." Human nature, even through Christians, always ends up getting in the way of God's plans.

Historically, the church has been slow to accept technological advances and to see their usefulness to Christians. The church in the fourteenth and fifteenth centuries did irrevocable damage by discrediting true scientists of that time. Some in the church even feared the printing press because of the possibility of its being used to spread evil, which it certainly has done. However, the tremendous opportunity it has given us to spread the gospel and make the Word of God available to the nations cannot be denied. Many in the church also resisted the use of radio, television, and the Internet for the same reasons. We cannot afford to put our heads in the sand and only make use of scientific advances after the world has used it for all the wrong purposes. We need to be visionary and look for opportunities to advance in discovery of knowledge that will be useful in the cause of Christ. We should never intentionally allow ourselves to be inferior or second-class in our ministries. We should pursue excellence in all that we do. If we keep our eyes on God and sift all things through His Word, we need not fear progress.

God called mankind to subdue the earth and exercise dominion over His creation (Genesis 1:26). One of our greatest opportunities to provide salt and light to our culture is through Christian education. We must not only believe in truth for ourselves, but we must stand up for it in the public arena. May we not neglect it.

In secularizing education, America has rejected the importance of truth. Because we have been too tolerant of worldly philosophies, they have taken captive the minds of our children. We have closed our eyes to advances of ungodly lifestyles. We have allowed people with evil intents to promote agendas that would legitimatize behavior that is detestable and abominable to God. We have allowed them to institute "diversity" and "tolerance" training in our schools that are, in fact, disguised attempts to create a social climate with no restraints on sexual behavior. We have stood by and wrung our hands while evolution teaching is forced upon our children, and they are taught the lie that it is all based on scientific evidence. We have allowed the government to muzzle any opposition that points out the fallacies and deceptions in the evolution theory. Because we no longer accept the concept of sin, we are unable to differentiate between right and wrong. Humanistic secularism has been trampling on truth for far too long. It is the mandate of Christians to contend for the faith, even if we are hated for it.

"The wrath of God is being revealed from heaven against all godlessness and wickedness of men who suppress the truth by their wickedness."

(Romans 1:18)

Truth About America's Troubled Soul

How can America turn back a violent, degraded, and immoral society?

Many Christians have become concerned about recent surveys that show very little difference between the private lives of those who claim Christianity and those who don't. George Barna's research has shown some disturbing results in the attitudes of church members toward morality. He found that over half of them believe co-habitation and sex outside of marriage are not necessarily wrong. About half think abortion is not a sin, and about a third see no problem with pornography or homosexuality. It has been known for some time that divorce rates among churched people are equal to or higher than the rest of society. It has been reported that the number one prayer request among pastors is the issue of pornography in their own lives. Barna's research showed the astounding evidence that about half of all Protestant pastors no longer hold a biblical worldview.

America has lost touch with the concept of sin. Our generation has defined sin as intolerance. We have been so immersed in a culture that no longer believes in eternal, unchanging truth that we have accepted the idea that each person can determine his own truth. This could only have happened by losing our conviction that the Bible is God's revealed Word and our source for knowledge of truth. The apostle Paul in his letter to the Romans reminded Jews that, "You have in the law the embodiment of knowledge and truth" (Romans 2: 20). In the book of Daniel, the angel in Daniel's vision said he would tell him "what is written in the Book of Truth" (Daniel 10:21).

Francis Schaeffer reminded his readers that "Christianity is not just a series of truths but Truth—Truth about all of reality." (1) As Schaeffer explained, liberal theologians have been trying for decades to mix two totally opposing worldviews, but in the final analysis where they always end up is on the side of humanism. This is what has led to the loss of a biblical worldview even among professing Christians. It has contributed to the breakdown of morality in our culture and will continue to do so unless churches return to teaching the truth, the whole truth, and nothing but the truth.

The godless philosophies that made their way into our universities at the beginning of the twentieth century got a firm foothold there by the middle of it, and made their way into high schools and elementary schools soon thereafter. The philosophical indoctrination of our children has now reached even into the preschool.

There was a time in the past when even in the public schools, America was acknowledged as a Christian nation. Days began with prayer, and teachers were free to quote the Bible as a basis for moral teachings. Ministers were expected to deliver the baccalaureate address to graduating seniors on the public school campus.

Things have changed catastrophically in the American soul. We can no longer call ourselves a Christian nation, and paganism's assault is whacking away continually at the minds of our children. Prayer is forbidden in our schools and biblical values have essentially been removed. Whenever anyone complains about the neglect of our Christian heritage, they are reminded that public schools are an arm of the government and as such must be separated from religion. We are told that our public schools must not elevate Christian ideals above those of Islam, Buddhism, Wicca, or Atheism.

Most Christians are thankful for and take comfort in the fact that there are many professing Christian teachers still in the public schools, at least in some parts of the country. Hopefully every Christian teacher is witnessing the love of Jesus to his or her students by the way they live and treat others. However, it is not nearly enough. The courts have declared that teachers cannot pray with their students, and they cannot talk to them about Jesus. They cannot read from the Bible as any kind of authority on morality, and they certainly cannot tell students how to be saved. When they encounter humanistic thinking in the curriculum that is contrary to the Bible, they are forbidden to tell their students the truth. Unfortunately many Christian teachers won't even recognize the error themselves because of the subtle indoctrination that has taken place throughout the culture and especially through their education.

Educators, even those who are Christians, have been

taught to fear any competition from private schools. In fact some are as hostile to Christian schools and home schools as the secular humanists themselves. Many of them say, "I believe in public schools" with almost the same conviction that they say, "I believe in God." A Christian acquaintance told me that his sister, a public school teacher and a professing Christian, believes that Christian schools are an invention of the devil. Though they must not realize it, these teachers have bought into the humanist philosophy that public schools are the salvation of our society. Some believe that the answer to our current moral crisis may be to have more Christian teachers in the public schools. However, many of them would also say that public schools must hold to the separation of church and state. The truth is that in public schools Christian teachers' hands are tied as far as ministering to students on a spiritual level. Furthermore, the percentage of teachers with worldviews in opposition to biblical Christianity has been growing rapidly.

We are told that the number one profession among New Age adherents is education. The percentage of homosexual teachers has also grown steadily. It is no secret that molesters and pedophiles are making their ways into the teaching profession as well. Education districts must now require that all applicants for teaching positions submit to fingerprinting and FBI and state bureau investigations before being allowed to teach or to work in any capacity with children in the public schools. In spite of this, stories of sexual abuse of students by teachers is a regular occurrence. A recent study commissioned by the United States Congress found that one in ten public school students claimed to have been victims of "sexual misconduct" by teachers or other school officials.

A few years ago a first grade teacher in Kentucky was arrested for prostitution. At about the same time, a junior high school teacher in another state was serving time in prison for seducing one of her students and becoming pregnant by him, not once, but twice. In 2003 a teacher was fired in California because she had been arrested for prostitution, but most people expected her to get her job back after an appeal. In 2004 a twenty-three-year-old teacher was arrested for having sex with a fourteen-year-old boy in the back of a car while his cousin drove them around. She told people she did it because she was turned on by the fact that it was illegal, but later claimed insanity as her defense. Around the same time, a forty-two-year-old teacher at an all boys Catholic high school in New York was arrested for having sex with several of the students. Since then news reports about sexual misconduct between teachers and students has been almost a weekly occurrence. Reports continue to surface about teachers whose pornographic pictures have turned up on Internet sites available to their students. It is obvious that in many of the nation's classrooms there is no longer even a climate of basic morality and decency.

There is no doubt that American families are in deep trouble. Our divorce rate continues to soar, and unmarried couples with families are a growing phenomenon. Many middle and upper class married people see nothing wrong with having extra-marital affairs, and thus no problem with leaving the marriage when they find someone else. Blended families are now commonplace. Children visiting biological parents only for weekends or vacations is the norm. Moms climbing the career ladder while their children grow up in daycare is a concern to some people, but not to most. It's just a fact of life in our society. There have even been studies to try to prove that children are not negatively affected by such. Even so, many mothers would gladly stay home with their children but find they can't because of the financial burdens brought on them by increasingly heavier taxes. Liberals claim we must have more and more tax dollars for education, welfare, and prosecution of criminals. Increase in criminal activity is not doubted, and we constantly face the problem of overcrowding in our growing numbers of prisons. We are told it costs more to keep a person incarcerated for one year than to send a child to college for four years.

Frustrated dads take to alcohol, become abusive, or simply walk away and leave their families behind. Out-of-wedlock pregnancies continue to soar. Abortion is casually used as a means of birth control, and women are legally allowed to have the brains of their unborn children sucked out and skulls crushed to make it easier for them to get rid of their babies. Incredibly, there is now mounting evidence that abortion causes extreme and gruesome pain to the fetus, yet the unborn are not even given sedation to decrease the level of torture. Our society has determined that spanking a child is violence against him and should not be allowed. We have also determined that capital punishment for the worst murderers is cruel and unusual punishment. As a nation, we seem to have no feeling whatsoever for the suffering of those in the womb, but feel it necessary to do away with any type of punishment for offenders in our society. What twisted reasoning we have produced!

We are dealing seriously with issues of infanticide, assisted suicide, euthanasia, and human cloning. There seems to be a sense of confusion about the role of family in our society and roles within the family. Family oriented ministries like Focus on the Family and Promise Keepers have been calling attention to the problems for several years and offering biblical solutions, but they are constantly attacked by liberal journalists and feminist groups.

A few years ago, a cartoon appeared in a local paper the day before Father's Day showing a mother and son in a card section of a store. The child was pointing to a section of cards labeled "Father's Day Cards" and asking his mother, "What's a father?" Probably no one was amused at the cartoon because surely most people realize there are all too many children in our country who could be genuinely asking such a question. There is no dad in their homes, and the schools certainly don't teach them about the role of a father. Surely the confusion about family roles has contributed to the number of children in fatherless homes.

In the same paper with the Father's Day cartoon was a column about the easy availability of pornography to children through the use of the Internet at their local library. A mother had brought suit against the library where her twelve-year-old son was able to access and copy sexually explicit materials. In her suit the woman asked that city officials be barred from using public money on the public library's computer system as long as such pornographic material was not blocked from use by children. Aiding the city attorneys in the case were the National Library Association and the American Civil Liberties Union. It is not surprising that the ACLU would take a stand to protect the library's "right" to keep indecent material available to children, but it should concern every one of us that the National Library Association with its close ties to education and involvement in the lives of our children should take such a stand.

It is no surprise that liberals would defend pornography on the basis of free speech. What is really disturbing is that so many Christian men and women find nothing wrong with it. Many of them know the words from Jesus that looking on a woman to lust means they have committed adultery in their hearts. Somehow they rationalize that they can look without lusting. This is a lie straight out of hell. Any knowledge of human sexuality recognizes that visual stimulation from a provocatively clad or naked body brings sexual pleasure. Lusting doesn't necessarily mean that a man desires to "have sex" with a woman. In getting sexual pleasure from looking at a woman's body, he is in a real sense already having sex. Some people also believe that what they look at has no effect on their marriage. This is foolishness. Men (and women) who view pornography build fantasies in their minds that become icons. No person alive can compete with a fantasy. The fantasy in reality has become an idol. The truth is that pornography has led many down a path that will eventually destroy their marriage.

Another very real indicator of the modern assault on the family is the growing disregard for human life. We hear frequently of parents killing their babies and dumping them in garbage cans. One of the most disturbing of those was of a high school girl a few years ago who gave birth in a bathroom during her prom. She callously left the dead infant in the trash and returned to the dance floor to dance with her boyfriend.

In January of 1999, a Shelbyville, Kentucky, man alerted police to the bodies of three tiny infants in his basement. Two had been wrapped and stored in boxes, and parts of the third were found burned in the fireplace. A man and his former girlfriend were charged with tampering with physical evidence and concealing the birth of an infant. No mention was made of a murder charge. It is unlikely that a murder charge would be made in the case of killing infants, especially when it is done by the mother because this is so connected to a woman's "right to abortion."

In recent times there have been a couple of news stories of fathers brutally stabbing their children. In one case the father not only killed his own child, but a friend of hers as well. Many of us will remember the cases of two mothers in the past few years. One mother sent her car into a lake with her two young children belted into their car seats and then told authorities they had been kidnapped. Another woman drowned her five children in the bathtub and then called police.

There have always been isolated cases of people killing their children, but not to the degree that we hear about it now, and more significantly not with the apathy from the courts and the public which we see today. How could any thinking person not make the connection between some of these killings and the growing acceptance of abortion on demand in this country? It is not a great leap from acceptance of the killing of the unborn to acceptance of the killing of the newborn. The truth is that there are a lot of people in this country who believe that a fetus is not a human being, and though they might be more reluctant to say so, some don't believe newborns are yet fully deserving of acceptance as persons.

Abortion has become one of the most "sacred" of human rights to many people in this country. When it comes to selecting judges to the Supreme Court, this is the most important litmus test on both sides of the political spectrum. The issue of abortion reached prominence only after the sexual revolution of the sixties. Concerned Christians must not lose sight of the fact that abortion is an extension of the sexual climate of the day, which is one of no boundaries, no restrictions, and no consequences for behavior. This permissive climate has given rise to a generation of people who surely are the most selfish and self-indulged human beings in history. They believe that nothing should stand in their way to getting whatever they want.

One of the strongest indictments of our nation's morality was the result of public opinion polls concerning the investigation of President Clinton for an alleged cover-up of a sexual affair with a young White House intern. According to the polls, most Americans believed the President lied about the affair under oath. Lying to a grand jury is a felony punishable by up to ten years in prison. However, most of those same Americans did not feel the president's behavior was an impeachable offense because it was all about sex. Some did not even feel it to be impeachable if the president had also attempted to persuade other witnesses to commit perjury in the case. Many in the media and in the government expressed anger and disgust toward the independent prosecutor for even investigating the alleged affair, and some defended the president. One talk show guest suggested that if there was a sexual affair, the only people it was important to were the president and his wife. Several suggested that when the special prosecutor finally presented his evidence to Congress, they would be unwilling to discipline the president because the public would be against it. The nonstop media talk about the details of the sordid affair only served to inoculate the public to any kind of shock or outrage that the president of our country was unfaithful, dishonest, a lawbreaker, and an absolutely terrible role model for our children.

When Congress did impeach President Clinton, the Senate was unable to get a two-thirds majority to convict him, even in the face of overwhelming evidence. Many Senators were unwilling to face a backlash from a public they believed was still loyal to a popular president. No doubt many of them couldn't convict him of something they didn't see as wrong. What this says is that Americans have become morally confused. What normally would draw outrage and certainly be punishable by law, suddenly took on a different judgment because it had to do with sex.

At about the same time that investigations of President Clinton were going on in Washington, a Legislative Research Commission in Kentucky was investigating allegations that the Director of the House Operations Office in the state capital had run a "travel business" out of his office through which he supposedly arranged outings for legislators complete with prostitutes and gambling for their enjoyment. There were rumors of topless women at golf events and of women put on the payroll because they agreed to have sex. (2) The director and three others were subsequently convicted of felonies. However, the commission found that although some legislators had acted boorishly, there were no crimes committed. Despite their finding no crimes by legislators, the commission recommended the adoption of more comprehensive rules governing social contact between legislators and staff members, including interns and other "temporary employees." (3)

Homosexuality is one of the biggest moral issues of our time and one that is systematically destroying what has been the basis of civilized society throughout history. Of course homosexuality has been around since the fall of mankind. However, because most societies have recognized its destructive powers, it has existed in the shadows much of the time. This behavior was at one time considered a mental disorder in America. That was a big mistake. It was only a matter of time before people would be ripe to accept it as merely an "alternative lifestyle." Since the sixties and seventies there has been an ever-increasing push in America to legitimatize homosexuality. In fact those who practice such behavior often try to pass themselves off as religious—even Christian, and much of our society is in agreement with them.

Logically there are only four possible explanations for justifying homosexual behavior. Either one doesn't know what the Bible has to say about it, has decided that God must have changed his mind, doesn't accept the authority of the

Bible, or doesn't care. The most likely culprit is the decision to discount the Bible as our source for truth. Many are willing to take bits and pieces of it to suit their own desires, but would never admit that it is either all the Word of God or none of it is. Some homosexuals seem to hate those who know what the Bible says on the matter, especially if they are willing to speak out publicly. What the Bible says about homosexuality is that God detests such behavior, and that it is indecent and perverse. (Leviticus 18:22–25 and Romans 1:24–27) Homosexuality is rebellion against God's natural creation and his purpose for man and woman, and therefore brings with it certain judgment. Romans 2:8 reminds us that "…for those who are self-seeking and who reject the truth and follow evil, there will be wrath and anger. There will be trouble and distress for every human being who does evil." In reading all the Bible has to say on the subject, one cannot escape the fact that homosexuality was included in the category of evil both in the Old and the New Testaments.

Why do homosexuals so loudly protest any use of the Bible in the debate? Some might say that it prejudices too many people against them, or that it doesn't take into account their belief that sexual orientation is inborn and that they have no control over it. However, if there is a God who created all humanity, as many of them would admit, wouldn't it seem inconsistent with his nature to condemn a behavior which he created in some people and over which they have no control? This leads right back to the question of whether or not one accepts the Bible as God's instruction manual. Does it have moral authority?

Homosexuality in the military had been taboo for most

our country's history, but one of the first things President Clinton accomplished in Washington was to institute a "don't ask, don't tell" policy. The president condemned Southern Baptists for their stand against homosexuality and praised the Disney Company for their "wholesome family entertainment," despite their sanction of same-sex partners as equal to the marriage relationship set down in the Bible. President Clinton even declared the month of June to be Gay and Lesbian Pride Month. As a part of his own campaign for president, Al Gore promised to make sure that gays would be allowed to serve openly in the military. In January of 2000, the Secretary of Defense ordered that all branches of the armed services institute training programs aimed at halting any and all harassment of homosexuals. While mistreatment and mean-spiritedness should be discouraged in all places, the new regulations could be interpreted as a green light for more homosexuals in the military, as well as leading to more blatant behavior. The policy would effectively silence the voices of those military leaders who recognize the detrimental affects that homosexuality would have on our country's readiness for conflict.

College campuses around the country have given gay and lesbian pride societies a green light for recruiting. Diversity and tolerance programs have now made their ways into many public schools. The problem is that due to the saturation of humanism throughout our culture we no longer have a moral consensus. Humanism made its inroads by way of our universities through acceptance of the theory of evolution and philosophies that proclaimed the death of God. The ultimate goal of these philosophies was the removal of restrictions on behavior, particularly sexual behavior and any feelings of guilt associated with them.

Professor Phillip Johnson, author of *Reason In The Balance,* often debates with evolutionists. He said, "I have found that any discussion about the weakness of the theory of evolution quickly turns into a discussion of politics, particularly sexual politics." (4) Most people who push so hard for the removal of the Ten Commandments from public places surely do so because they want no reminders of the wickedness in their own lives. The Bible says that wicked people avoid the light because their deeds are evil, and they don't want it to be exposed. Homosexuality has now attempted to become openly acceptable, but they still fear the light of God's Word. That is why they try to discredit the Bible and silence anyone who brings it up.

Secularists have not been content to remove the Ten Commandments from school walls. The Boy Scouts of America have been under attack for several years because of their refusal to accept known homosexuals into leadership roles. They have also been criticized because they have refused to take God out of their creed. The American Civil Liberties Union has even pushed to restrict the Scouts from using any public facilities. Humanists want no trace of God or his laws left in our society, and they will not be content until America is a totally secular society. Why? Because their deeds are evil.

America has become so sold out to the god of sex, that nothing is any longer considered out of bounds. At the same time, there seems to be an epidemic of dysfunction among the male population if one is to believe the commercials.

Products claiming to be cures for sexual dysfunction must be selling plenty and making millions of dollars. When Scott Peterson was arrested trying to flee the country after killing his pregnant wife, among the things he packed for the trip was a good supply of Viagra. Ravi Zacharias, in his book *Cries Of The Heart,* said, "Any pleasure, however good, if not kept in balance, will distort reality or destroy appetite." (5) Sex is unquestionably one of those areas of life that is badly out of balance in our culture.

A look at today's entertainment shows that same preoccupation with sexual license. Profanity, nudity, and sex acts are common in movies like *Sin City* and *Wedding Crashers,* which gross millions of dollars in a single weekend. Much of the music listened to by teens and preteens have blatantly obscene sexual lyrics. Very disturbing is the fact that the listening and viewing habits of kids growing up in Christian families is much the same as those of their peers who have no religious inclinations.

Our news is filled with stories of sexual crimes against children. Sexual predators kidnap, abuse, and murder children throughout the nation. In one such story in the summer of 2005, a known sex offender first killed a mother, one of her sons, and her boyfriend in order to kidnap her two younger children. After sexually abusing both children for several weeks, he killed the nine-year-old boy before being caught with the eight-year-old sister. That was only one of several such stories that captured nationwide attention during that same summer. There were also several news stories about judges who refused to punish sexual offenders by sending them to prison. One judge, who had several drunk-driving incidents himself, said that a sexual predator of children had a sickness and therefore shouldn't be punished. Several states refused to remove judges who could no longer carry out just sentences. Those same legislators could not bring themselves to pass laws requiring mandatory sentences for sexual predators.

Reasoning people have to wonder why so much of the breakdown of our society involves sexual attitudes and behaviors. According to the Bible, it is because God intended human sexuality to be a vehicle for producing godly offspring (Malachi 2:15). For that very reason, it would be a target of the devil for continuing his rebellion through mankind. Jesus said in John 8:44 that the devil "is a liar and the father of lies." The problems in our society that come from sexual misconduct and perversion reached their prominence on the back of lies.

Those of us who are concerned about the moral condition of our society cannot allow ourselves the leisure of ignoring the political issues of our day. Christians cannot hide behind the church doors any longer. We have to take a stand against those who threaten the sanctity of marriage, the sanctity of life, and the religious freedoms of this nation. We must do this in spite of the anger and attempts at humiliation and retribution that will come from the other side. We must hold our leaders accountable, and we must fight the humanistic stranglehold on America's education system. We must become critical thinkers who examine the issues by holding them up to the light of eternal truth. Then we must act. If we do not, we will have failed to follow our Lord's command to be salt and light to our generation.

Salt is a preservative that can be used to keep things from rotting, and light exposes the destructive things that have been hiding in the darkness. May God help us to be willing to be what He called us to be.

God gave the responsibility for raising and educating children first to parents. They will ultimately be held accountable for their children. It is crucial for Christians to develop in our children a distinctly Bible-centered Christian view of life and a lifestyle consistent with that view if we are to be a positive influence on our society. However, it is becoming increasingly clear that for most of us this objective cannot be realized in the context of public schooling at this time. It is inevitable that compulsory education funded by government money will be politicized, and those factions that have the most political clout will succeed in force-feeding their ideas to the next generation.

In our complex society it is very difficult for most parents to consider home schooling, and private Christian schools can be expensive. However, parents still must determine the education their children will receive. There are several options open to parents who recognize the importance of training their children in the nurture and admonition of the Lord. Christian schools are becoming more available all the time. Most provide scholarships of some kind. There are young and older teachers who would love the opportunity to do the home schooling for a group of parents. Those who feel their only option is to continue in the public schools have a much greater challenge in monitoring what is taught to their children. They must keep in mind that it is not just the textbooks they need to keep an eye on. They had better be willing to search out the worldviews of those who instruct their children as well as the worldviews that subtly pervade the curriculum. They must prepare their children in advance to recognize false worldviews and give them the tools to defend their own.

Public schools are expected to teach multiculturalism, diversity, and religious neutrality through equal elevation of all religions when religion is acknowledged at all. Actually, in many ways public schools treat religion as irrelevant. The textbooks no longer portray America as a religious nation, and our founding fathers, if mentioned at all, certainly are not portrayed as men of true faith in God. Their characters and morals have been called into question. Revisionist history is fast replacing traditional history in many schools. Particularly disturbing are books and videos that portray America as aggressors using religion as an excuse to overpower defenseless people. Anti-American sentiment has been escalating among the liberal crowd in our nation for some time. It is especially high among college professors and journalists (including television anchors) who use their bully pulpit to turn unsuspecting young people in that direction. Francis Schaeffer warned that television news had the potential to influence and become a part of the political process itself. He said, "We must realize that the communications media function much like the unelected federal bureaucracy. They are so powerful that they act as if they were the fourth branch of government in the United States." (6) Schaeffer said that even CBS commentator Walter Cronkite expressed concern over whether or not democracy could continue to be a "suitable philosophy" in a generation that is so vulnerable to media. (7)

Though we have to be careful not to over-spiritualize everything, there is good reason to believe that every problem our nation faces and every threat to our democratic way of life can be linked to false philosophies that have taken control of our thinking. Every failed program in public schools, whether it is the teaching of reading and math or sex education and wrong-headed self-esteem efforts, is somehow tied into flawed philosophies. Everything in life does begin and end with the spiritual. There is a reason why some things build up and others tear down. This universe works in an orderly fashion because an orderly God created it. That same orderly Creator has spoken ultimate truth. He has told us that wisdom, knowledge, and understanding come from him. When that truth is denied, anything built on the resulting philosophy is inevitably going to fail. Not only will it fail to produce what it promises, it will bring destruction to the soul. Those responsible for forcing these philosophies on our culture did so to remove all boundaries to and any feelings of guilt for their personal pleasure. However, as Ravi Zacharias reminds us, "Ultimately meaninglessness does not come from being weary of pain, but meaninglessness comes from being weary of pleasure." (8) Solomon discovered the same truth, and many more since then have found at the end of pursuit of pleasure they are bankrupt in their souls and can see no reason to live. Ravi Zacharias said, "All pleasure is built upon why you and I exist in the first place. Life…must be defined first, and on the basis of that definition we are to make the right choices that will truly delight and not destroy." (9)

Due largely to the philosophical takeover of public schools by those who claim to be progressive, America has seen a continuous trend toward secular humanism and a near-mortal blow to our faith. We have lost the conviction that ultimate truth exists and that it is important to the health of our nation. We are living in a violent, degraded, and rapidly demoralizing society. We are soul sick and becoming sicker.

Our nation can no longer be considered a Christian nation. If there is any hope of a turnaround, it will come through changed hearts and minds. Only the message of truth through Jesus Christ can accomplish this. Therefore, the only hope that we have for the continued blessings of liberty and the pursuit of happiness must come through a return to the faith of our fathers. Our public education system is now a tool in the hands of immoral forces, and, unfortunately, a lot of churches have been so contaminated with secularism that they are no longer avenues of truth.

Worldviews are important, for they determine the goals for an individual, an organization, or a society, and the means one is willing to use to meet those goals. It is important that we recognize our worldview and how we acquired it. It is important to know how the philosophies underlying our worldview hold up next to reality and in the light of truth. If they are false, they will lead to destructive and disastrous consequences, just as certainly as designing a bridge on wrong physical assumptions will lead to its collapse.

America is now guilty of the same heinous crimes

against God's laws that brought destruction to other societies. Can we expect God to overlook it because we are America? The book of Proverbs tells us that "evil men do not understand justice" (Proverbs 28:5). It also declares that "if anyone turns a deaf ear to the law (God's law), even his prayers are detestable" (Proverbs 28:9). As a nation we have surely turned a deaf ear to the law, and it appears that our prayers must have become detestable to God. Only as Christians begin to turn away from their own wicked ways in repentance will we be able to pray for revival and hope to be heard. God help us to recognize where we have been, where we are, and why, and to turn our hearts toward Him before it is too late.

ENDNOTES

Looking for Truth in Education
Can education which ignores truth be a noble enterprise?

1. Jay Cooperider, "Teaching in all its forms takes center stage," PURDUE UNIVERSITY PERSPECTIVE, Spring, 1998.

2. Whittaker Chambers, *Witness,* New York, Random House, 1952, p. 269.

3. Ibid.

4. Ibid.

5. John Dewey, "New Republic," Nov./Dec., 1928, p. 86.

6. Francis A. Schaeffer, *A Christian Manifesto,* Wheaton, Illinois, Crossway Books, 1981, p. 17.

7. Ibid, p. 25.

8. Ibid, p. 29.

9. James Dobson and Gary Bauer, *Children at Risk: The Battle for the Hearts and Minds of Our Kids,* Dallas, Texas, Word, 1990, p. 19–20.

10. Sharon Begley, "A World of Their Own," Newsweek, May 8, 2000, p. 55.

11. Ibid, p. 63

12. Elaine Fletcher, "Study: society's attention toward

religion declining," "Western Recorder," March 21, 2000, Vol. 177, No. 12.

13. Adelle Banks, for Religion News Service, "Western Recorder," May 9, 2000, p. 13.

14. Whittaker Chambers, *Witness*, New York, Random House, 1952. p. 83.

15. Ibid, p. 149.

16. Ibid, p. 195.

17. Jennifer P. Brown, "Judge: Futrell trial on," "Kentucky New Era," August 4, 1998, p. A1.

18. Michael Quinlin, "Auditor assails education agency," "The Courier-Journal," Louisville, Kentucky, April 19, 2000, p. A6.

Truth and Liberty, the Connection
Is there danger in forgetting the source of freedom

1. David Barton, *Original Intent, The Courts, The Constitution, and Religion,* Aledo, Texas, Wallbuilder Press, 1996, p. 182.

2. Ibid.

3. Ibid, p. 79.

4. Ibid, p. 86.

5. Ibid, p. 131.

6. Ibid, p. 173.

7. Ibid, p. 153.

8. Ibid, p. 152.

9. Ibid, p. 156.

10. Ibid.

11. Kathleen Parker, "Parents squarely to blame for teacher-terror violence," Kentucky New Era, Hopkinsville, Kentucky, June 11, 1998.

12. Whittaker Chambers, *Witness*, New York, NY, Random House, 1952, p. 83.

13. Ibid, p.16.

14. Francis A. Schaeffer, *A Christian Manifesto*, Crossway Books, Wheaton, Illinois, 1981, p. 49.

15. Ibid, p. 71.

16. Ibid, p. 79.

Philosophy and the Test for Truth
Was God holding out on Adam and Eve?

1. C.S. Lewis, *Mere Christianity*, New York, N.Y., Touchstone, 1996, p. 21.

2. Ibid.

3. George Johnson, "Science and Religion: Attempts to bridge the great divide," The Courier-Journal, Louisville, KY, July 5, 1998.

4. Lee Strobel, *The Case for Christ*, Grand Rapids, MI, Zondervan Publishing House, 1998, p. 260.

5. Ibid, p. 240.

6. Paul Little, *Know Why You Believe*, Downer's Grove, IL, Inter Varsity Press, 1988, p. 123.

7. John Dewey, "My Pedagogic Creed," Essay, *The School Journal*, Vol. LIV, No. 3, January 16, 1897, pp 77–80.

8. "Humanist Manifesto II," American Humanist Association, *Humanist Magazine*, 1973.

9. Ibid.

10. John Dewey, "My Pedagogic Creed," Essay, *The School Journal*, Vol. LIV, No. 3, January 16, 1897, pp 77–80.

11. The Reader's Digest Great Encyclopedic Dictionary, Pleasantville, N.Y., The Reader's Digest Association, Inc., 1975.

12. Ibid.

13. Lonnie Harper, "School guide drops word evolution," The Courier-Journal, Louisville, KY, October 5, 1999, p. 1.

14. James Glantz, "Poll: Americans favor teaching creationism and evolution," The Courier-Journal, Louisville, KY, March 12, 2000, p. A7.

15. Ibid.

16. Ibid.

17. Phillip E. Johnson, *Darwin on Trial*, Downers Grove, IL, Inter Varsity Press, 1993, p. 10.

18. David A. Noebel, *Understanding the Times*, Colorado Springs, CO, Association of Christian Schools International and Summit Ministries, 1995, p. 84.

19. Ibid.

Truth or Consequences
Is education tied to the rise of rebellion, depression, suicide, and immorality in America's youth?

1. The Reader's Digest Great Encyclopedic Dictionary, Pleasantville, NY, The Reader's Digest Association, Inc., 1975.

2. Charles Wolfe, "Davies schools find music hones brains," Kentucky New Era, Hopkinsville, KY, June 16, 1998.

3. Peter Kreeft, *The Best Things in Life*, Downers Grove, IL, Inter Varsity Press, 1995, p. 99.

4. Ibid.

5. "Maine Youth at Risk," http://www.acadia.net/emnc/suime.htm.

6. Sheila Norman-Culp, "Hesse's book adds somber note to summer reading," Kentucky New Era, Hopkinsville, KY, July 3, 1998, pp B5-B6.

7. Ibid.

8. Ibid.

Truth About Change
Is there really anything new in education?

1. Encyclopedia of Education Research, 6th Edition, Vol. 2, p. 428.

2. Larry McShane, "Media credibility takes another

blow with CNN apology," Kentucky New Era, Hopkinsville, KY, July3, 1998., p A3.

3. Clarence Page, "Drudge doesn't look so bad after the media retractions: Kentucky New Era, Hopkinsville, KY, July 15, 1998.

4. Ibid.

5. Ibid.

6. Frankfort, Kentucky (AP), "Officials: Schools unprepared to handle growing problems," Kentucky New Era, Hopkinsville, KY, July 9, 1998.

Truth About Our Shifting Culture
Does education hold the power to change the worldview of a nation?

1. Phillip E. Johnson, *Reason in the Balance, The Case Against Naturalism in Science, Law and Education,* Downers Grove, IL, Inter Varsity Press, 1995, p. 166.

2. Ibid, p. 123.

3. Ibid, p. 171.

4. Charles Colson and Nancy Pearcy, *How Now Shall We Live,* Wheaton, IL, Tyndale House Publishers, Inc., 1999, p. 190.

5. Ibid, p. 183.

6. *The Kentucky Education Reform Act, A Citizen's Handbook,* 1994 Edition, pp 5–9.

7. *Kentucky Teacher,* August, 1994, p. 24.

8. David Karem, "An ear for improving KERA," The Courier-Journal, Louisville, KY, Jan. 2, 1996.

9. Camille Wagner, *The Kentucky Citizen,* Nov./Dec., 1993, Vol. II, No. 6, p. 3.

10. Ibid.

11. *KERA Briefing Notebook, An Update by the Partnership for Kentucky School Reform,* May 1993.

12. Encyclopedia of Education Research, 6th Edition, Vol. 2, p. 428.

13. Ibid.

14. "Task Force on High School Restructuring, Final Report," June 30, 1993, p. 12.

15. "Assumptions and Beliefs of the Task Force," *KERA Briefing Notebook, An Update by the Partnership for Kentucky School Reform,* May, 1993.

16. Ibid.

17. Ibid.

18. Bill Adcock, "Too many errors without explanation," The Messenger, Madisonville, KY, July 30, 1996.

19. "Task Force on High School Restructuring, Final Report," June 30, 1993, p. 12.

20. Frankfort, Kentucky (AP), "State sets new standards for classroom specialists," Kentucky New Era, February 18, 1999.

21. Raphael Nystrand, "Preparing teachers in a era of

reform," The Courier-Journal, Louisville, KY, Dec. 12, 1995.

22. Ibid.

23. Ibid.

Truth in Testing
How do we know what children know?

1. *Kentucky Teacher,* August, 1994, p. 19.

2. Ibid.

3. Lucy May and Bob Geiger, "Kentucky fourth graders show no improvement on national reading test, Lexington Herald-Leader, Lexington, KY, April 28, 1995.

4. Mark Shaver, "State's school boards call standards misdirected," Louisville Courier-Journal, Louisville, KY, June 30, 1994.

5. Ibid.

6. Donna Shedd, "Anyone paying attention to KERA gate?" The Messenger, Madisonville, KY, Feb. 21, 1996.

7. Charles Wolfe, "Portfolios fail panel test," The Messenger, Madisonville, KY, June 28, 1995.

8. Ibid.

9. Mark Shaver, "Teachers' poll links test gains to coaching," The Courier-Journal, Louisville, KY, August 16, 1996.

10. Associated Press, "State allegedly ignored complaints

about cheating on school tests," Louisville Courier-Journal, July 11, 1997.

11. Associated Press, "Jessamine schools' test scores set at zero," Kentucky New Era, Hopkinsville, KY, Nov. 21, 1997.

12. Charles Wolfe, "Panel mulls education challenge," Kentucky New Era, Hopkinsville, KY, July 7, 1998.

13. Kent Ostrander, "Kentucky's NAEP test fiasco," The Kentucky Citizen, Vol. VI, No. 4, July/August, 1999.

14. Lonnie Harper, "Group says state must improve reading skills," The Courier-Journal, Louisville, KY, June 23, 1995.

15. Ibid.

16. Bruno V. Manno, Hudson Briefing Paper, Indianapolis, IN, Hudson Institute, No. 165, June, 1994, p. 11.

17. Ibid, pp 11–12.

18. Mark Shaver, "Report could make KERA test more traditional," The Courier-Journal, Louisville, KY, June 23, 1995.

19. Donna Shedd, "Anyone Paying Attention to KERA gate?" The Messenger, Madisonville, KY, Feb. 21, 1996.

20. Francis A. Schaeffer, *A Christian Manifesto*, Wheaton, IL, Crossway Books, 1981, 20.

21. Ibid. p. 21.

22. Ibid, p. 24.

23. Ibid, p. 25–26.

24. Ibid, p. 45.

25. Ibid.

Choosing Truth in a Worldview
What difference does our belief system make?

1. David Noebel, *Understanding the Times*, Colorado Springs, CO, Association of Christian Schools International and Summit Ministries, 1995, p. 15.

2. Ibid, p. 2.

3. Ibid, p. 26.

4. Chester E. Finn, Jr. and Diane Ravitch, "A report from the educational excellence network," edexcellence. net/library/epctoc.htm/

5. Ibid.

6. Robyn Blumner, "Vouchers intended to destroy public schools," The Journal Gazette, Fort Wayne, IN, June 16, 1998.

7. Ibid.

8. Ibid.

9. Andrew J. Coulson, "The Wisconsin Supreme Court ruling on the Milwaukee Government Voucher Program," 1998, www.schoolchoices.org

10. Ibid.

11. Susan Okie (The Washington Post), "Tots now

get drugs to alter emotions," The Courier-Journal, Louisville, KY, Feb. 23, 2000.

12. Francis A. Schaeffer, *A Christian Manifesto,* Wheaton, IL, Crossway Books, 1981, p. 34.

13. Ibid, pp 33–34.

Trampling on Truth
What lies led to a crippled America?

1. Jonathan Wells, *Icons of Evolution,* Washington, D.C. Regnery Publishing, Inc. 2000, p. xii.

2. Ibid, p. 220.

3. Ibid, p. 221.

4. Ibid. p. 223.

5. Ibid, p. 91.

6. Mona Charen, "Gays Manipulate public opinion," The Courier-Journal, Louisville, KY, January 27, 2000.

7. Ibid.

8. Ventura, California (RNS), "Barna claims U.S. Christians stuck in a rut," The Western Recorder, March 13, 2001, Vol. 175, No. 10.

9. The Gallup Organization, Princeton, NJ, "Six in ten Americans read the Bible at least occasionally," www.gallup.com, copyright 2006.

Truth About America's Troubled Soul
How can America turn back a violent, degraded, and immoral society?

1. Francis A. Schaeffer, *A Christian Manifesto,* Wheaton, IL, Crossway Books, 1981, p. 20.

2. Editorial, "Legislators come out OK in this scandal," Kentucky New Era, Hopkinsville, KY, July 20, 1998.

3. Ibid.

4. Phillip E. Johnson, *Reason in the Balance The Case Against Naturalism in Science, Law, and Education,* Downers Grove, IL, Inter Varsity Press, 1995, pp 46–47.

5. Ravi Zacharias, *Cries of the Heart,* Nashville, London, Vancouver, Melbourne, Word Publishing, 1998, p. 140.

6. Francis A. Schaeffer, *A Christian Manifesto,* Wheaton, IL, Crossway Books, 1981, p. 60.

7. Ibid, pp 59–60.

8. Ravi Zacharias, *Cries of the Heart,* Nashville, London, Vancouver, Melbourne, Word Publishing, 1998, p. 128.

9. Ibid, p. 132.